The Eucharistic Visions of St. Frances of Rome

THE EUCHARISTIC VISIONS OF ST. FRANCES OF ROME

Translated by Fr. Robert Nixon, O.S.B.

SOPHIA INSTITUTE PRESS
Manchester, New Hampshire

Cover design by Updatefordesign Studio.

Cover photograph provided by the translator.

Sophia Institute Press
Box 5284, Manchester, NH 03108
1-800-888-9344
www.SophiaInstitute.com

paperback ISBN 979-8-88911-390-4
ebook ISBN 979-8-88911-391-1

Library of Congress Control Number: 2024952018

First printing

To faithful Benedictine oblates throughout the world

Contents

Translator's Introduction

St. Frances of Rome (1384–1440) is a remarkable and radiant figure among the pantheon of Catholic saints, and she has inspired love and veneration ever since her own time. A mystic, visionary, and industrious helper of the poor and the afflicted, she combined the vocations of a faithful and competent Catholic wife and mother with that of a devout woman of consecrated life.

She was born into a wealthy, illustrious Italian family, and although she felt called from an early age to offer herself to God as a nun, her family determined that she should be married. She accepted this decision as the will of God, manifested through the circumstances of her life, and in a spirit of holy obedience, and she served as a good, dedicated wife to her husband (who was also a man of outstanding wealth and nobility) and as a wise, gentle mother to her children. Nevertheless, she continued to follow a demanding regimen of prayer, devotion, and evangelical simplicity consistent with that of consecrated religious life.

Her charitable activities included working in several of the hospitals of Rome, where she gently tended to the most wretched cases. She offered hospitality and charity also to the multitude of beggars who inhabited the city, and her door was always open both to the destitute and to the spiritually afflicted.

A group of other devout women sprang up around St. Frances, inspired by her example, and joined her in prayer and in works of mercy. Eventually, she established a convent of remarkable beauty and splendor for these holy women, known as the Tor de' Specchi (Tower of Mirrors), which continues as a convent in Rome to this day. One of the unique features of this convent was that it was a community of Benedictine *oblates*—that is, persons who do not take solemn religious vows but commit themselves to living according to the Rule of St. Benedict in a manner consistent with their own state of life. Today, there are many thousands of Benedictine oblates throughout the world, and St. Frances of Rome is regarded as their foundress and special patron.

Through much of her life, St. Frances experienced remarkable visions and revelations. Many of these visions occurred after her reception of the Holy Eucharist. In the fifteenth century, most Catholics received the Eucharist only once annually, but Frances received it much more frequently, as the recorded visions collected here attest. Her reception of the Blessed Sacrament was always preceded by Confession, penance, fasting, and prayer and followed by devout meditation and thanksgiving.

These Eucharistic visions offer beautiful insights into the power and significance of the great Sacrament of the Body and Blood of the Lord, and they illustrate in an unforgettable manner how the Sacrament serves as a foretaste of the glories of Heaven. The visions are rich in symbolism, and many are filled with profound theological and mystical illuminations. The mystical images they present can hardly fail to inspire divine love—especially for Christ Jesus, truly present in the Sacrament—in the hearts of all those who read them. For this reason, the present translator humbly suggests that they are particularly apt for reading and meditation in preparation for receiving or adoring the Most Holy Sacrament of the Altar.

Fortunately, St. Frances had a wonderful spiritual director, Canon Giovanni Matteotti, who diligently kept records of all that Frances shared with him. After her death, Matteotti compiled these in writing, in Latin. These writings, collected in the *Acta Sanctorum*, published in Antwerp in 1668, are the source of the translation that follows.

Included also in this volume are a summary of the wonderful life of this saint and a description of some of the frightening demonic attacks she experienced. These were all carefully committed to writing by the same Canon Matteotti.

It is the hope of the translator that the writings that follow may help to highlight for contemporary Catholic readers the beauty, splendor, and infinite love of the Divinity Himself, who is truly, really, and substantially present—in veiled form—in the great Sacrament of the Body and Blood of Our Lord Jesus Christ; to whom be glory and honor forever and ever. Amen.

Fr. Robert Nixon, O.S.B.
Abbey of the Most Holy Trinity
New Norcia, Western Australia

The Life of St. Frances of Rome

Written by Canon Giovanni Matteotti, her spiritual director

St. Frances was born to a noble, illustrious Roman family in the year of Our Lord 1384. Her father was Paolo Bussa, and her mother was Iacobella dei Roffredeschi, both of whom were persons of good and pious life as well as very prosperous and distinguished status. They were both still in their early years and in the flower of youthfulness when they conceived Frances, the servant of God. Their daughter, even from her earliest days, was radiant with many wondrous and remarkable virtues, bestowing luster on the whole city of Rome by her sanctity and goodness. Indeed, she shines forth like the morning star through the clouds of darkness in which our present times are engulfed.

When she was still an infant, Frances gave many signs of her future sanctity. Even as a toddler, she would not permit herself to be touched by any man, no matter how closely related to her, with the single exception of her father. As she grew up, she never participated in the childish pranks and futile games and jests of other children her age. Rather, she preferred to remain at home, devoting herself to prayer, fasting, and other works of piety. This she did assiduously, both day and night. Until she reached the age of eleven, she lived virtually as a hermit, and, as a consequence, her existence was virtually unnoticed even to the near neighbors of her household.

When she reached her teenage years and began to mature as a female, the love of holy chastity for the sake of the Kingdom of God grew steadily in her. Filled with devotion and holy aspirations, she fervently wished to remain a virgin dedicated to God alone. Her father, however, would not consent to this intention but instead committed her to marry a certain wealthy nobleman. Shortly afterward, this arrangement was formalized, and Frances was married.[1]

Struck with disappointment over being unable to follow what she felt was her vocation, Frances suffered a very severe illness. Her malady incapacitated her to the point where she became utterly unable to move and so was confined to her bed. Many distinguished physicians were consulted, but they were completely unable to bring about any improvement in the afflicted girl. Instead, Frances's illness persisted for a very long time without improvement.

Having given up hope in the abilities of the physicians, some of her neighbors eventually engaged the services of a certain old woman who practiced witchcraft. This woman asserted that she

[1] St. Frances was married to Lorenzo Ponziani, a commander of the papal military forces, at the age of just twelve. Arranged marriages were usual among noble families at the time. Marriages occurring at such early ages were generally not consummated immediately, but often after a delay of some years, and were effectively 'binding engagements.' It should be noted that marriages did require the free consent of the persons being married at this point, and, even if they took place primarily out of obedience to parents (as was the case with Frances), the persons concerned were not forced or compelled to such obedience.

would be able to restore Frances to health by means of her various occult arts. But Frances was appalled at this impious and wicked scheme and fervently drove the witch from her presence.

The night after this happened, St. Alexius of Rome appeared to Frances.[2] The soul of this venerable saint asked her, "Do you wish to be healed, Frances?" Upon seeing this vision and recognizing the saint, she replied to him joyfully: "Yes, indeed! But only if it is the will of God." And the very next morning, Frances arose perfectly well, her health fully restored! At once, she hurried to church, to give thanks to God and make her confession.

Having fully recovered from her prolonged illness, St. Frances began to direct her attention to caring for others who were afflicted, either by illness or by poverty. For thirty years, during which time she remained a faithful wife in the household of her husband, she devoutly served in "Santa Maria in the Chapel," a hospital for the sick and the destitute that was located in the trans-Tiberian district of Rome. Frequently she would bring food to the most wretched inmates of this hospital, often supplying it at her own expense. Indeed, she would tenderly clean the wounds and sores of those suffering from the most repulsive ailments and afflictions, washing with her own noble hands the filthy rags they wore.

Frances served the afflicted not only in practical ways but also by giving them spiritual consolation and encouraging them to be strengthened and reconciled through the sacraments of the

2 St. Alexius of Rome was born to a wealthy Roman family in the fourth century. To escape an arranged marriage, he fled to Syria and lived as a beggar for many years. Later, he returned to Rome and his family's household. They did not recognize him after so many years of absence, however, so he worked as a servant for them for several decades. It was only after his death that they discovered that this "servant" was, in fact, the long-lost son.

Catholic Church. She performed such works of devout piety also in various other hospitals of Rome, including the Hospital of St. Cecilia, the Hospital of the Holy Spirit in the Sassia district of Rome, and the Hospital that is called the "Holy Field."

From her girlhood until the very end of her life, Frances lived under strict obedience to her spiritual father.[3] There was nothing, however arduous or demanding, that her spiritual father enjoined her to do that she did not fulfill, not only readily but joyfully and enthusiastically. She exhibited this virtue of obedience to all others and strongly commended it—both by word and example—to the sisters who were under her spiritual guidance.

Now, Frances fervently desired to lead a life of solitude so that she could devote herself purely to contemplation of the glory of God without any distractions. She had a chapel built in her house, and in the gardens of their residence she set up a kind of grotto under the branches of an apple tree. In these places, it was her custom to dedicate herself to prayer and holy meditation in silence and solitude.

Once, in the month of April, when the trees were in blossom, as Frances meditated in this grotto, she reflected on how the ancient Desert Fathers used to live off the roots, leaves, and fruits that nature provided for them. And as she thought thus, two ripe apples appeared on the tree above her and fell to the ground—despite the fact that it was not yet the season for such fruit! In fact, the tree bore at that time nothing but leaves and blossoms. This event caused great wonder and amazement, and both Frances and other members of her household enjoyed the miraculous fruit from the tree.

[3] This was Canon Giovanni Matteotti, who is the author of this biography.

Such was the humility of St. Frances, the servant of God, that she considered herself and described herself as nothing other than a vessel of impurity, and as one filled with the filth of vice. Although she was now the wife of an extremely rich and noble husband, she preferred to clothe herself in extremely simple and inexpensive garments. Indeed, from her youth she had treated with disdain gold, jewelry, and all the other usual items of womanly ornamentation.

And although she was of a household that was filled with riches and abundance, she would often go forth into the streets of Rome dressed in the poorest and humblest of clothing and beg for alms on the streets. This she did to cultivate humility, and she would give all the alms she had gained to the genuinely needy and destitute. For example, on a certain day when a plenary indulgence was granted to all the faithful who visited the Basilica of St. Paul, she remained on the steps of this great church from dawn until evening in the company of the beggars of Rome, imploring alms from the generosity of all who passed by.

Another way in which she raised money for the poor was by collecting sticks and branches, which could be sold as tinder to the residents of Rome. Frequently she could be seen carrying bundles of sticks through the streets, sometimes bearing them upon her head and other times upon a donkey that she kept for this purpose. She would often collect fallen sticks and branches from her family's vineyard outside St. Paul's Gate of the city, to sell as tinder to raise alms for the destitute.

There were many servants and maids in the household of her husband, and Frances conducted herself toward these with the utmost humility, affability, and kindness. Indeed, she was less like a demanding mistress among them and more like one of their coworkers, referring to them all as her brothers and sisters. If she unintentionally offended any of them or caused them pain, she would immediately fall to her knees and ask for forgiveness, as is the custom among monks and nuns. But if any of the servants happened to say something incautiously that was offensive to God or to His saints, she would firmly correct their impiety and irreverence.

She managed the domestic matters of the household of her husband and family diligently and as befits a good Catholic wife. The virtue of patience was her constant crown and adornment, and she bore all adversities and difficulties with quiet faith and courage. In the time of war, she endured with almost incredible patience all the injustices and pains that resulted from the conflict and the violence. This included not only the loss of property and livestock but even the tragic death of her own beloved son.

Throughout her life, Frances not only meekly accepted and tolerated the cruel and false words of her detractors and opponents, but she even prayed for such wicked people. In suffering such persecutions and calumnies, the servant of God rejoiced, for she felt that, at such times, the words of the Apostle St. Paul could justly be applied to herself: "For Christ's sake, I delight in weaknesses, in insults, in hardships, in persecutions, in difficulties."[4]

It was not only from malicious and ill-willed human beings that this servant of Christ suffered attacks, but evil spirits and demons also often afflicted her. These evil spirits and demons would appear in various forms, including as lions, dogs, serpents, human beings, and angels. Often these evil spirits would lift her high above the ground and then cast her down violently; and

[4] 2 Cor. 12:10.

at other times, they would beat her fiercely and unrelentingly. After St. Frances had established her convent, the sisters of her community often witnessed such things visibly. They clearly saw her being raised into the air and cast down and heard her being beaten. But the demons themselves remained invisible to all, except to Frances herself.

These evil spirits often urged or tempted her to wrong or imprudent actions. But fortunately, Frances was blessed with the gift of discernment and so was always able to recognize their attempted deceptions, and accordingly she refused them firmly.

Once it happened that Frances was devoting herself to prayer, sacred reading, and meditation in a place especially set aside for this purpose. Now, by chance, there happened to be a large pile of ash in that chamber. Various evil spirits were also lurking there. Assuming the forms of different malign beasts and frightening creatures, these evil spirits fiercely attacked the servant of God. These demons tore apart the prayer books that were there and viciously beat St. Frances, rolling her body in the pile of ashes. So wounded and besmirched was she that her form hardly appeared human at the end of this terrible and terrifying encounter with the forces of darkness!

That night, as Frances prayed in her chapel, a demon again attacked her. This time it seized her by the hair and lifted her up, holding her suspended in the air from a nearby balcony for a considerable period. It threatened not to release her unless she consented to its vile temptations. But when St. Frances firmly refused, strengthened by the power of God, the wicked demon eventually gave up and returned her to her place of prayer unharmed.

Frances experienced many such attacks from demons and evil spirits during her life, but she always emerged from them victorious and unscathed.[5] For no torment, trap, or temptation, however terrifying or dire, could separate her from her faith in Christ and her wholehearted love for Him. She remained invariably constant and unwavering, confiding in the Lord and confident that He would bring about saving fruit even through the difficulties of her adversities and trials.

Frances's attention, kindness, and generosity were always directed toward the poor and the needy. Indeed, she even opened her home to them as if it were a public place of respite and shelter. Never did a poor person approach her for help and not depart from her fully satisfied. Frances would even empty the haversacks of the homeless, removing the wretched, rotten food they had managed to collect and filling them instead with good-quality, nutritious food from her own kitchen, sometimes even adding desserts and treats as an extra kindness. Hence it was that God deigned to perform marvelous works of mercy through His faithful servant Frances, even while she remained a diligent wife in the household of her husband.

On one occasion, when the summer heat was particularly oppressive and the supplies of wine were running very low throughout the city of Rome, many of the poor, the destitute, and the afflicted came to her. They begged her, for the love of God, to supply them with some wine with which to parch their thirst. Now, there happened to be a large jug of fine wine in the cellar of Frances's house. This jug of wine had been placed there by her husband's father, who had given instructions that it was to be kept

[5] Many of these experiences of demonic attacks are included in the appendix of this work, "The Demonic Attacks Experienced by St. Frances of Rome." Again, these were related by Frances to her spiritual director, Canon Giovanni Matteotti, who recorded them carefully.

in reserve for him and his son. But Frances, being tenderhearted and filled with compassion, could not refuse the desperate pleas of the poor; and so she gave them some wine from the jug. And because those who were in need were very many and extremely thirsty, it was not long before the jug, which had been filled with fine wine, was completely empty!

Later, the father-in-law of Frances, together with her husband, visited the cellar, expecting to drink from the jug of wine that had been placed there in reserve. As might be expected, the father-in-law was enraged and the husband was also greatly vexed when they discovered it to be completely empty! Both of them reproached Frances angrily for letting this happen, since the cellar was her responsibility as matron of the house. She tried to quell their anger with mild words and an explanation of what had happened, but in vain.

So, with full confidence in the power of God, she prayed over the empty vessel for a little while, and, when she arose from her prayer, the jug was found to be filled to the brim with wine. And this new wine was of even finer quality than that which she had given away!

News of this miracle quickly spread throughout the whole neighborhood, and all marveled at the grace of God manifested through the prayers of His handmaid, St. Frances.

Another time, a famine afflicted Rome and the area around it, resulting in a widespread shortage of grain. Frances's husband had sold most of the family's reserves of wheat for a considerable profit, so nothing remained in their own granary except for a few stray leftovers. But Frances knew that the local poor were severely afflicted by hunger, so she took the little grain that remained and gave it to them generously. But however much she gave, the granary never seemed to run completely empty. Even after a few days of her generosity, there was found to be no less than forty pounds of quality wheat still remaining—more than there had been at the beginning.

Such was the ardor of the charity that filled the heart of Frances, the spouse of Christ, that she endeavored to provide not only physical sustenance for the poor but also spiritual nourishment for souls in need of it. Whenever she noticed someone who was spiritually discouraged or struggling to resist vices and temptations, she strongly encouraged them and exhorted them with loving care, just as a kindly mother encourages her own children. She prayed devoutly for all those whom she knew to be in need of her prayer, placing her own welfare and happiness always as a secondary consideration to that of others.

Hence it was that, with the cooperation of divine grace, Frances saved the souls of many from the snares of the enemy of the human race, by means of both her words and her example. For her very presence, which exuded angelic innocence and goodness, was enough to refresh the heart of the dejected and to encourage those whose virtue or faith was wavering. Her words flowed like delightful honey to those who heard them and wondrously inflamed in all her hearers both the love of God and disdain for worldly temptations. Whoever was dejected or depressed or felt that temptation was getting the better of them could seek out Frances and be sure of receiving consolation, encouragement, and inspiration from her.

Furthermore, this devout servant of God succeeded in resolving many feuds and disputes and quelling scandals and seditions of all kinds. Long-standing hatred and animosity she managed to extinguish by means of the peace, charity, and compassion that she constantly sowed. And those whom she converted to love of God and neighbor were many indeed.

From the time of her youth until the end of her life, St. Frances had a custom of visiting churches very frequently and hearing Masses, sermons, and the prayers of the Divine Office with great devotion. She carefully retained in her memory the saving commandments and precepts of the Lord as well as the teachings of the holy Catholic Church, and she endeavored always to fulfill these faithfully and to the best of her ability. She invariably showed sincere reverence and honor to persons in the ministry of the Church, including secular clerics, members of religious orders, and priests. Such was her deference to these ecclesiastical persons that she barely dared to speak in their presence, but rather, genuflecting and with eyes cast to the ground, she would venerate Christ present in the person of His ministers.

Every week, and especially on Sundays, she would diligently make her confession. Under the instructions of her spiritual father, she would devoutly receive the Body of Christ in the Holy Sacrament of the Eucharist, filled with fervent love and devotion. Often, after she had received the Blessed Sacrament, a sweet fragrance miraculously filled the entire chapel where she was present.

On one occasion, when Frances presented herself to receive the Body of Christ, a certain excessively officious priest at the Basilica of St. Cecilia, with presumptuous temerity, judged it to be unfitting that a married woman such as St. Frances, and especially one who was well endowed with worldly riches, should receive Holy Communion so frequently. So this priest gave her an unconsecrated host instead of the genuine Body of Christ. But this attempted deception was immediately noticed by Frances, the servant of God, who experienced none of the spiritual sweetness that normally accompanied her reception of the Sacred Eucharist.

The spiritual father of Frances, when he found out what had happened, reprimanded the priest both for his presumptuous judgment and for his attempted deception. And the misguided priest immediately recognized his error and earnestly pleaded for mercy.

Blessed Frances offered prayer in a manner that was tireless and unceasing, doing so always with a joyful and attentive soul. Each day, she would devote time to sacred meditation, often augmenting this with further meditation during the hours of the night. It was rare for anyone to come to visit her and not to find her occupied with fervent prayer and devotion. Each day, she would pray the Office of the Blessed Virgin Mary and recite many other psalms and prayers. With great fervor, she engaged in sacred reading and delighted greatly in hearing the words of Sacred Scripture read aloud.

There were numerous miraculous manifestations of the power and efficacy of the prayer of St. Frances. Once it happened that a certain woman from the Arezzo region of Italy, Bartolomea by name, visited the convent that Frances established for her spiritual daughters. She saw a beautiful golden rod, ornate with lilies, descending from the heights of Heaven and hovering over the room of St. Frances, who was then engaged in prayer and divine contemplation. Filled with amazement, she cried out and pointed out the miraculous vision to the sisters of the convent who were there, and they all witnessed this mystical sign.

Another time, St. Frances and the sisters of her convent were in their vineyard, engaged in tending the vines and picking grapes. Frances stopped her work for a while to pray her daily Office of the Blessed Virgin. Then a storm suddenly broke out, and rain began to fall heavily. Now, there was no shelter or covering of any kind in the vineyard, so all of the sisters were soaked by the rain. But Frances, who stood there praying her office, was entirely untouched by the rain, with not a single drop falling upon her, even though she stood in the middle of the field with no shelter of any kind.

While Frances was still living in the household of her husband and he was still alive, a congregation of devout women gathered around her, thanks to the grace of almighty God. Later, she built a convent for them, known as the Monastery of the Tor de' Specchi [Tower of Mirrors]. These women, together with St. Frances herself, committed themselves to observing the rules of religious life set down by the Olivetan Congregation of the Order of St. Benedict. And Frances and her sisterhood of other devout women observed the Rule of St. Benedict faithfully for the remainder of their lives. This new community, which was based on the observance of the Rule of St. Benedict and involved private commitments as Benedictine oblates[6] rather than any solemn religious vows, was given the official approval and blessing of Pope Eugene IV.

St. Frances lived with her husband for some twenty-eight years and six months. But, by common agreement and mutual consent, for twelve years of this time they abstained from conjugal relations.

[6] Benedictine oblates commit themselves to living according to the Rule of St. Benedict in a way that is consistent with their status in life. They do not take solemn monastic vows and are not obliged to renounce property or nobility rights and so forth. In the time of St. Frances, many widows—including those with children, even adult children—would not have been able to make formal monastic vows but may have felt called to live a religious life. There were also a variety of other reasons why it may not have been possible for a person to make formal vows (such as the disruption or loss of the hereditary rights of a family or uncertainty about one's final vocation).

The spiritual delight that Frances took in heavenly contemplation was so great and her spiritual union with Christ was so strong that very often she would be taken up into states of mystical trance and lose consciousness of the external world. During this time, she would typically be rendered completely motionless, remaining thus until her ecstasy or vision came to an end. This frequently occurred after she had devoted herself to prayer and meditation, and especially after her reception of the Most Holy Body of Christ in the Eucharist. But it also occurred after her meditation before a crucifix and after her conversations on holy matters with her spiritual father.

During these periods of mystical trance, Frances would often become so still and immobile that she seemed to those who observed her to be dead rather than alive. In one instance, on the vigil of the solemnity of the apostles St. Peter and St. Paul, as she returned from the Basilica of St. Paul, she paused for a while on the bank of a certain river or stream for sacred meditation. There, she entered a state of deep trance. Then, rendered immobile, she fell into the river! She remained floating in this stream for several hours, until the sisters of her community found her. Naturally, they were shocked and horrified. They carefully took her out of the water, hoping and praying that she had not drowned. But, to their surprise, not only was she perfectly well, but her clothing and her body were completely dry, as if utterly untouched by the waters of the stream.

St. Frances often received the Sacrament of the Body of Christ in the Chapel of the Holy Angels in the Basilica of Santa Maria in Trastevere in Rome. Frequently, as she prayed and meditated after the reception of the Blessed Sacrament, she would enter into a state of trance and experience remarkable and wonderful visions. Sometimes even before receiving the Sacrament, she would be drawn into a state of trance and proceed to the altar to accept the Body of Christ while in this mystical ecstasy. The spiritual daughters of St. Frances who accompanied her would often observe a radiant light shining over the head of this blessed soul as she prayed devoutly, either before or after receiving the Blessed Sacrament.

It was with the most intense compassion and love that Frances meditated upon the sufferings and Passion of Christ. She would often burst into freely flowing tears as she thought of Our Lord's agony and death. As she meditated devoutly on each of His sacred wounds, she seemed to feel the pain of those wounds herself. These meditations would render her completely incapable of performing any of her normal duties or activities, so that all she could do was lie on her bed in stillness.

Once it happened that, as Frances contemplated the sacred wound on the side of the crucified Christ, the Holy Spirit touched her with a fire of compassion and love that was so ardent that a wound miraculously appeared on her own side. For a long space of time, liquid continued to flow from this wound without cessation. Eventually, on the solemnity of the Nativity of the Lord, St. Frances received the Eucharist in the aforesaid Chapel of the Holy Angels. Then, taken up into a trance, she had a vision of the Blessed Mother of God, adoring the divine Son whom she had borne. As she beheld this vision with joy, the long-lasting wound in St. Frances's side was instantly healed.

Frances, the servant of Christ, also continually experienced visions of angels. One particular angel of remarkable beauty was visible to her constantly, both day and night. The face of this angel was of such radiance that it exceeded the brightness of the sun. If, for any reason, Frances had to perform some task in the darkness of the night, she had no need for any physical lamp, for the light that emanated from her angelic companion's face was more than sufficient to illuminate her way.

When she had come to the fifty-second year of her life and her husband had passed away, she felt called to renounce the world entirely. With the most profound humility, she went to the convent occupied by the sisters who were her own daughters in Christ, which she herself had built for them. With outstretched arms and flowing tears, she implored them to accept her as one of their sisters. This, of course, was something to which they joyfully agreed, for St. Frances was regarded as a kindly and holy mother to the entire community.

In the year of Our Lord 1440, on the second day of March, a severe fever suddenly struck Frances, who was now in the fifty-sixth year of her life. That night, it was revealed to her that, within the space of seven days, she was to depart from her earthly dwelling place. The next morning, she revealed this to her spiritual father and humbly requested from him the final sacraments of the Church. Having been strengthened by these, she gathered to her all the sisters of her community. With maternal affection, she offered to them words of consolation and encouragement, urging them to cultivate divine love and to preserve with diligence sisterly charity among themselves. She exhorted them to bear all tribulations and trials with fortitude and constancy, to spurn the temptations of the enemy of the human race, and to follow faithfully, with the help of God's grace, in the footsteps of their Lord and God, Jesus Christ.

And so, after the seven days had passed, on March 9, 1440, in the company of her spiritual daughters and sisters in Christ, St. Frances, the most devout spouse of Christ, fell asleep in the Lord, leaving behind the light of this earthly sphere. She did so with her eyes fixed serenely upon Heaven, and fervent prayer both on her lips and in her heart. And her blessed soul, released from the bonds of the flesh, was taken up into the heavenly abyss of eternal glory and love, for which she had always fervently longed.

The Eucharistic Visions of St. Frances of Rome

Recorded by Canon Giovanni Matteotti, her spiritual director

Vision 1

April 1431

On a certain day, St. Frances, the handmaid of God, received the Most Holy Body of Christ with the greatest prayerful reverence and awe. This took place in the small but beautiful and ornate Chapel of the Holy Angels, in the great Basilica of Santa Maria in Trastevere in Rome. It was then about the hour of midday, and the sun glowed brightly outside. After reception of the Blessed Sacrament, Frances remained in devout silent prayer and meditation for a considerable while, and during this time her soul was taken up into a state of mystical ecstasy. And while in this mystical ecstasy or trance, her whole body remained completely and perfectly still.

After Frances had returned to her natural senses and her trance had ended, she was diligently questioned by her spiritual father, Canon Giovanni Matteotti, under holy obedience, about what she had experienced and witnessed while she was in this state of trance. Filled with reverence, she humbly replied to him that after receiving the Blessed Sacrament, she was filled with an immense and indescribable joy. She was led in spirit into a vast and beautiful meadow, filled with a multitude of diverse plants of a most splendid and noble nature.

In the middle of this verdant meadow, there was a wonderful fountain, perfectly round in shape and fashioned from a material similar to the finest alabaster. It had steps of gleaming white all around it. From the heavens there descended upon this fountain an abundance of the sweetest waters, of crystalline clarity and the most brilliant purity. Wherever these waters fell, radiant brightness would sparkle forth in a rippling and variegated array of light and iridescent color. These mystical waters bedewed the whole field in refulgent splendor, flowing forth from the fountain as gentle but lively streams. And wherever these waters touched the grasses or plants, they caused flowers and blossoms of the most incredible beauty and wondrous variety to spring up and bloom.

Then St. Frances saw seven beings in human form approach the fountain in order to drink from it. When she saw this, she, too, was filled with burning eagerness to drink from its crystalline and shimmering waters. As she longed for this so avidly, a single precious drop of these living waters fell into her mouth. She then felt a satisfaction and consolation that were so delightful that it was scarcely able to be believed, and the joy she felt surpassed all imagination and desire.

Having drawn closer to the fountain, she then perceived the following words carved upon it in gleaming letters of brilliant gold:

> The Lord of love, through tender grace,
> Shall draw to His divine embrace
> Each soul that burns with love for Him
> And purifies itself from sin.

St. Frances would have desired to remain there longer; but, though she was unwilling, the vision then ceased once she had read these words. While she was in her ecstasy, she had said, in the hearing and view of both her spiritual father and her spiritual daughter Rita: "I implore You, my Lord, who are the perfect abundance of love, if it is Your will, to liberate my soul from all its anxieties and worries, that I might find peace in You alone."

This took place in the month of April of the year of Our Lord 1431.

Vision 2

April 1431

On another occasion, after receiving the Most Holy Sacrament of the Body of Christ in the aforesaid Chapel of the Holy Angels in the Basilica of Santa Maria in Trastevere in Rome, Blessed Frances was again taken up into a trance for the space of about an hour. This took place while she was engaged in silent prayer and meditation. While in this trance, it was as if her soul had been taken up into the glorious realms of Heaven, while her body remained perfectly immobile here on earth. Indeed, she did not move at all, except for some very slight motions of her eyelashes at times.

After this time, movement returned to her body, although she remained in a trance-like state. She then uttered the following words:

> O most fervent Love, do not betray me, nor permit me to depart from You, nor send me away in my pains! I wish no more to stand without You, most merciful Love. Do not send me back into the darkness of the world, for I am no longer able to tolerate it. At the very least, tell me why I must be separated from You!

All of these words were clearly heard by Frances's spiritual father, Canon Matteotti, and also a certain daughter of hers in the Faith, named Rita, who often accompanied her to church. Once Frances had returned to her normal senses, this same spiritual father directed Frances to reveal to him her vision.

She responded, under holy obedience, that she had been led in spirit to a brightly shining pillar of immense size, standing on the peak of an extremely high mountain. The top of this brilliant pillar was so high that it seemed to touch the heavens themselves. And from the top of the pillar a blazing fire issued forth. St. Frances understood this brilliant fire to represent divine love. As the holy fire went forth, it divided itself into a great many parts. One of these parts of the flame went up and entered Heaven. Another encircled the high mountain upon which the pillar stood, illuminating it with a magnificent splendor and luminescence. Another part of the fire divided itself further and entered into the great multitude of people who were gathered there.

This multitude of people were assembled around the base of the pillar, and they were divided into four distinct groups. When the fire of divine love approached one of these groups, they flatly refused to accept it. And—alas—this group remained in their darkness and filth, cloaked with a murky mire of sin and ignorance. The fire then descended upon another group, but the people of this group chose to ignore it and turned their backs to it. Upon a third group of people, the holy fire then descended. This third group did accept it, but only half-heartedly and with certain careless tepidity.

The fire then descended upon the fourth and final group, who embraced the flame from the pillar with great honor and enthusiasm. These were the people who accepted the love of Christ with genuine faith and devotion. But Frances noticed that this final group, who fully and lovingly received the flame of divine love, were only very small in number compared with the other groups.

When her spiritual father questioned her about this in more detail, she told him that those who were in this last group, which received the fire fully, were only about one in a hundred, compared with the whole multitude gathered.

She related also that, as she stood at the base of the pillar, she heard a voice going out and proclaiming: "I am Love! I love those who love me, and I make their love grow and become strong and unwavering. I am the holy Love which makes the soul capable of receiving love, while it knows it not."

This vision took place in the month of April, in the year of Our Lord 1431.

Vision 3

Solemnity of the Most Holy Trinity 1431

On another occasion, St. Frances received the Sacrament of the Body and Blood of the Lord, in accordance with her spiritual father's instructions to do so. This took place in the same Chapel of the Holy Angels mentioned previously. After reception of the Sacrament, St. Frances remained completely immobile in her body for the space of about an hour. And after this, her natural senses returned to her, and she regained her usual consciousness.

When asked by her spiritual father, Canon Matteotti, what she had experienced and witnessed during that time, she said that her spirit had been led on high and positioned in an amazingly splendid temple. This temple was of a magnitude and beauty so immense and glorious that it could scarcely be compared to any edifice on earth.

Into this magnificent temple there descended a certain person from Heaven, of most brilliant and radiant appearance, whose name was "The Burning Tabernacle." This tabernacle opened itself to Blessed Frances, though it had no door. The spirit of Frances, the handmaid of God, then entered into the mysterious depths of this celestial chamber, filled with unspeakable joy and wonder.

And while her spirit remained in this tabernacle, she heard a song of incredible soaring harmonies and smelled an unknown fragrance of the most ineffable sweetness. She experienced there such joy, peace, fulfillment, and sweetness as no human mind could imagine. As she herself attempted to describe this to her spiritual father, words almost failed her.

Within the tabernacle, St. Frances perceived that there was a basin filled with very precious and beautiful objects and jewels and glowing with the color of pure gold. Her spirit was filled with an eagerness to take or to taste some of these precious and mysterious treasures. But, although she longed to do this with the most avid desire, she found that her hands were not able to take hold of anything—as if some unseen force prevented them from doing so. So, boldly and taking courage, she immersed her whole head into this basin! And she tasted therefrom a single drop of the unfathomable glories that were within it. The taste of this small drop delighted her spirit with such an intensity that it exceeds all possible comprehension.

After she had narrated all of this, Frances entered a mystical state once more and heard a voice speaking to her. It said: "O happy soul, be firm in your faith! Do not waiver. Consider continuously all that Love has done for you, and all the toil it has sustained for such a long time for your sake. The world hated and despised the One who fulfilled all that the Scriptures and the prophets had spoken of Him. Be strong and committed to your holy resolve! Love Itself has paid your price and redeemed you.

"And look further," the voice continued, "and behold how Love has positioned Itself in a high and fitting place, so that It may receive you to Itself and embrace you! Blessed soul, guard yourself, lest thieves break in and maliciously betray you. Be steadfast in your love of God and never recede from it."

Having heard these words, while still enrapt in ecstasy, she said (in the clear hearing of her spiritual father, Canon Matteotti, and her spiritual daughter Rita):

> O Lord, do not send me away from You! For my heart is painfully torn and wounded with great bitterness. Do not permit me to perish, for I am scarcely able to live anymore! Sometimes I feel that it would befit me to depart from this wretched earthly life. Without You, my own abilities and virtues are not able to raise me up. You alone are able to renew me, O God, according to Your holy and wise will. O sweetest Love and Lord, do with me what only You are able to do! Grant light to my heart and fullness of grace to my soul, so that I may become pleasing and acceptable to You.
>
> Oh, if I have to leave You, my poor heart will be broken. I shall be unable to do anything at all, and, without You, I will not be capable of standing firmly by my own virtue and strength, for I am feeble and weak.

Frances spoke these words with the utmost anguish. Yet, despite her words, her spiritual father did not believe that she was really in peril of physical death.

This vision occurred in the year 1431, on the solemnity of the Most Holy Trinity.

Vision 4

Feast of St. Mary Magdalene, July 22, 1431

Following reception of the Divine and Most Holy Sacrament in the aforementioned Chapel of the Holy Angels, the spirit of St. Frances, the handmaid of God, was again taken up into mystical ecstasy, and she entered a trance-like state. During this time, her body remained completely immobile for the space of an hour, after which she returned to her natural senses. Her spiritual father, Canon Matteotti, then asked her, under religious obedience, to describe to him all that she had experienced and witnessed during the time when her normal consciousness had left her. She related how she had been taken up into a great light and, from there, had been taken into another light. This second light was even more vast than the first one and shone with an unearthly refulgence that surpassed anything she had ever experienced.

In this celestial light, Frances saw a very beautiful and ornate tabernacle, with three small drums positioned nearby. Upon this tabernacle there was a Lamb of incomparable radiance and whiteness. And there were three flocks of other lambs who were approaching it, all displaying indescribable joy and frolicking happily. As they approached, they made joyful, dance-like movements in chorus before the great Lamb upon the tabernacle. As they passed by that great and holy Lamb, they each would humbly display their reverence and adoration, by bowing their heads or kneeling to the ground. These three flocks of lambs each took to itself one of the three drums positioned near the tabernacle.

While the body of St. Frances remained perfectly still, she heard the Lamb of incomparable whiteness and beauty speak to her. It said:

> I am that Love who gives forth the fragrance of the fruits that flourish in my eternal and celestial homeland! After the soul experiences this fragrance, I then give it a foretaste and a flavor of these heavenly fruits, which is delightful beyond all imagining and which satisfies every desire and longing of the heart.
>
> And after this [the radiant Lamb continued], such souls become strangers to all worldly cares and ambitions, and they burn with love for Me alone. From then on, they do all they can to find the One who caused them to feel such love. They strive to strip themselves of all else and all earthly concerns. Humbly, they consider themselves as nothing, denying their own will and appetites. Indeed, they even long to undergo trials, they yearn for martyrdom, and they submit themselves humbly and gladly to the yoke of holy obedience; all so that they may be more perfectly united to the One who has filled them with such passionate and incomparable love!

Then her spiritual father, Canon Matteotti, and the aforementioned Rita heard Frances speak clearly, despite the fact that she was still immobile and in a state of trance. She said:

> I wish to remain with You always, and I do not intend to depart from here ever! Surely, a person who has been

> invited to a place as a guest should not be violently cast out. Oh, why do You wish to make me again search for that which I now possess and enjoy so wonderfully? I wish to waste no more time on my earthly pilgrimage, lest my sloth become harmful to me. Rather, I wish to remain with You forever and never to be parted from Your glorious presence! It is You who are the Creator of mind and heart, and it is You who bestow upon them their capacities and desires. And, therefore, these ultimately can find their satisfaction in You alone and in nothing else!

Thus it was that the soul of St. Frances longed to remain in her mystical state and enjoy forever this blessed vision of love and joy she had been granted forever. Indeed, she did not wish to re-enter into the weight of her physical body and the concerns of her earthly life.

At this point, she heard a resonant and harmonious voice of great power and sweetness saying: "If anyone thirsts, let him come to Me and drink!" And then the Lamb of most radiant and pure appearance turned its chest toward the other lambs assembled around it, with a most loving and beautiful expression. It gestured to them to drink from its chest, which was opened with a great wound. These other lambs, with a look of peace and delight, ran to it eagerly and drank from the open wound upon its chest.

The spirit of St. Frances was also led with these lambs. She gazed into the wound upon the breast of the Lamb and perceived there something like a vast ocean of infinite light. As she saw this, she was filled with a longing not only to drink from the open wound but to enter fully into it. And she seemed to be given permission to do so; but somehow she was held back from entering as she wished. Yet, as she gazed longer into the deep ocean of light, her desire to enter it became ever more ardent and compelling, until it almost overwhelmed her.

At this point, she heard a voice saying, "I am that Love who says, 'If anyone thirsts, let him come unto Me and drink.' Yes, I wish to satisfy all who come to Me in love and humility, and I have opened My own heart so that I am able to receive you as My beloved and special guest."

This vision took place on July 22, 1431, the feast day of St. Mary Magdalene.

Vision 5

August 1431

On another occasion, when St. Frances, the handmaid of Christ, had received the Most Holy Body of Christ, she was praying devoutly (as was her custom) in the Chapel of the Angels, in the Basilica of Santa Maria in Trastevere. Once again, the spirit of the saint was taken up into a mystical rapture, while her body remained immobile in a trance-like state for a considerable period.

When later questioned under holy obedience by her spiritual director, Canon Matteotti, St. Frances related that, in her spirit, she had been transported to a vast plain or field that was wonderfully illuminated with brilliant light. This field was of incredible beauty, its grass glowing with the rich verdure of a precious emerald. And in that field was a wondrous Lamb, whose fleece shone with a radiance exceeding that of the purest snow. Standing close by this Lamb (which was very manifestly none other than the divine Lamb of God) was a noble youth of great delicacy and beauty. He wore upon his shoulders a garment resembling a dalmatic and a crown woven of flowers and laurels rested upon his head. Surrounding the divine Lamb was also a chorus of other figures in human form, wearing beautiful vestments of a variety of colors and crowned with roses. These human figures (whom

Frances recognized to be the souls of the saints) were paying devout homage to the Lamb and exulting jubilantly in Its presence.

The aforementioned youth, wearing the dalmatic, appeared to be leading all the others. As they passed before the Lamb, with great jubilation and devotion they sang thus:

Let us all the Lamb adore
With joyful hearts, for evermore;
Let us to His glory sing,
For He alone is King of kings!
His love He promised to impart
To each and every humble heart:
This love is our supreme reward,
And this pure Lamb, our only Lord!

St. Frances perceived also that there were several streams or rivulets that flowed through this field of astonishing beauty. Each of these streams—which were five in number—flowed with waters of a different color. The noble youth who was vested in the dalmatic led Frances, together with the chorus of the saints, to each of these rivulets in turn and explained the symbolic meaning of each.

The first of the streams flowed with waters of rich red, which glowed with the roseate luster of a precious ruby. And the angelic youth here exclaimed, "Behold, this first ruby-hued rivulet represents the ardent and invincible love with which Christ redeemed the human race. For it was in the crimson stream of blood that flowed from His wounded side that salvation poured forth for the world!"

The next stream was filled with a liquid of a milky-white color, which shone like polished ivory or newly fallen snow. And the youth here said, "This second stream, of immaculate purity and untainted clarity, represents holy innocence. For it is innocence and purity of conscience alone that may ascend the holy mountain of God, to behold there the supreme goodness of the Creator!"

The third stream flowed with waters of shimmering verdant green. "These are the waters of hope," exclaimed the youth, "for hope is the virtue that imparts vitality and fertility to all the good and perfect things for which love strives!"

The fourth stream was filled with waters of bright azure blue, resembling the color of the vault of heaven on a cloudless, sunlit day. The youth vested in the dalmatic said, "This stream represents the virtue of holy obedience, which leads the soul on the gentle ways of righteousness and brings it finally to blessed and blissful union with the divine will."

The fifth stream was crystal clear and perfectly transparent without any hint of coloring at all, like a precious diamond without fault or flaw. "These transparent and clear waters are the stream of purified faith, unpolluted by any taint or cloud of doubt and fear, and as strong and inviolable as a faultless diamond. The soul that drinks of these waters of perfect faith and that immerses itself in their crystalline purity shall never be separated from the highest beatitude of divine glory!"

At this point, as Frances related, her vision came to an abrupt end, and she found herself once more in her mortal body, in the chapel in which she had been praying. She was then filled with bitter anxiety, and desolation and sorrow that her most glorious vision had been terminated so suddenly.

"Alas," cried the saint sadly, "I have been cruelly deceived! For in my heart, I firmly believed that I would remain in that place of splendor and beauty forever, but now I have returned to this earthly valley of tears and the drab dreariness of mortal life. Yet I know that God never deceives anyone."

At this point, a certain evil spirit suddenly became visible to Frances. She then realized that it had been this malign entity that had implanted in her mind these dangerous feelings of anxiety and bitterness. So, calling upon the grace and mercy of God, she was able to dispel this wicked demon, together with the dark emotions he had generated. And, having done so, she gave thanks and praise to her loving Lord for revealing to her in this vision a most wonderful foretaste of the beauty and splendor of the celestial Kingdom that awaited her in the future.

Frances experienced this vision in the month of August, in the year of Our Lord 1431.

Vision 6

January 20, 1432

Another time, after St. Frances, the servant of Christ, had received the Blessed Sacrament in the same Chapel of the Holy Angels in the Basilica of Santa Maria, she entered into a state of deep mystical trance. Afterward, when she had returned to her natural senses and her normal consciousness, she revealed to her spiritual father, Canon Matteotti, under holy obedience, all the details of the vision that she had experienced while in her state of trance.

She related how she had been taken to the time before the angels had been created, for it had pleased God to grant to her a vision of His divinity in this primordial state. Frances saw an immense circle, perfectly round, and of such extreme brilliance and intense luster that she was barely able to look upon it. Beneath this radiant circle, there was a space that seemed to be a vast, limitless void. This great void was filled with something that was like air but was not air. Within the vast, brilliant circle, there was a large image or statue of a dove, of incredibly pure and sparkling whiteness.

For St. Frances, the handmaid of God, this radiant image of a dove was like a mirror of the face of Christ. Looking at this statue of a dove, as if gazing into a looking glass, she was able to perceive there the full glory of the Divinity. She saw also on its gleaming surface the following letters inscribed: "The Beginning that has no beginning; the End that knows no end."

She then comprehended that before anything at all was created by God, all things existed already as conceptions and forms in His divine mind and that He willed to create them in order to manifest and give expression to His omnipotent and incomprehensible wisdom.

The blessed soul of St. Frances saw next the creation of the angels. These were all created simultaneously in a single moment. Their multitude was such that it could be likened to the fall of glistening and beautiful snowflakes on a lofty mountain peak in wintertime. But immediately the vast multitude of angels assumed an ordered arrangement, with the newly created angels assembling themselves in perfectly harmonious hierarchy within their respective choirs. And St. Frances was able to perceive and understand the dignity and glory of each of the particular angelic choirs.

The saint perceived next the separation of those good angels who were destined to remain in grace from those who were doomed to fall and thus to be expelled from their heavenly glory. She saw that those who were doomed to fall were about a third of the total multitude of the angels, while those who were destined to remain in a state of grace were about two-thirds of the total number.

In her vision, St. Frances witnessed how the celestial Queen, the chosen Mother of the only-begotten Son, was conceived eternally free of Original Sin, in accordance with the will and plan of God.

Looking further at the radiant likeness of a dove, as if gazing more deeply into a mirror, Frances saw there more letters, inscribed as if in a circle. They read:

I am that noble and fruitful Love who grants liberty unto the soul; I make it to be filled with love, and grant to it perfect understanding, making it comprehend all things that were created for it, before it even came into existence!

It is I who illuminate the human mind, that it may see the truth; I have created it rational and have bestowed upon it My own holy Name. I have created humanity so that they may enjoy glory, not so that they may be kindred with the beasts. They were made to occupy My celestial Kingdom, taking the place of those angelic spirits that have fallen. I created each human being to possess eternity, yet—alas—many have acquiesced with the devil, rather than with Me! Through wicked pride, many have sought to know and to obtain that which befits them not; and so, through this same pride that brought about the ruin of angels, they too have fallen!

This vision occurred in the year of Our Lord 1432, on the twentieth day of January.

Vision 7

February 1432

Having received once again the precious Sacrament of the Body of Christ in the same Chapel of the Holy Angels already often mentioned, St. Frances, the handmaid of God, was taken up once more in spirit into a mystical trace. During this time, her body remained immobile, but later resumed its normal mobility when she returned to her natural senses. Her spiritual father, Canon Matteotti, questioned her under holy obedience concerning what she had seen. And Frances told him how she had seen the Lord and Savior in His most sacred humanity. He bore in His side a wound, but as the saint looked upon this wound, it took on the likeness of a great ocean of profound depth.

As Frances gazed into this deep ocean, inflamed with the fire of compassion and love for the Lord, a divine voice came forth from the depths of the waters. It said, "I am ardent Love, and I suddenly draw unto Myself the soul that loves Me. Then I place it in a realm where it will live forever in Me, Jesus, its Redeemer."

As this point, Frances was almost overcome with an intense love and longing for Jesus. She felt her sins disappear from her soul, as if by being washed away, and her heart become inflamed with a holy love of indescribable sweetness. It was as if she had entered into an abyss of delight, filled with indescribable treasure, while she herself was transformed by and united with God's eternal and unfathomable beatitude.

She then heard the words of St. John the Evangelist being spoken by a resonant voice from on high. This celestial voice proclaimed, "In the beginning was the Word, and the Word was with God, and the Word was God."[7] Upon hearing it thus spoken, St. Frances somehow felt that she then understood this mystical verse completely and to its very depths, with a kind of mystical enlightenment that was beyond all human explanation and all intellectual teaching.

After this mystical revelation, while Frances was still in a state of trance, she heard another voice speaking to her. It said,

> I am the pure and noble font! If anyone thirsts, let him come unto Me. And whoever wishes to come to Me shall receive from Me a joy that has no end. Humility combined with purity of obedience, and love combined with a clean conscience join themselves together in a strong, unbreakable bond. Whosoever cultivates these will be able to drink deeply from this font.
>
> O soul, know that the virtue of holy poverty may be divided in a triple way. If your soul desires to be guided and to follow with all its heart the guidance it will receive, it will very quickly arrive at the goal to which it aspires. It will be able to sustain any worldly conditions and circumstances, as long as it remains in a state of sincere humility.
>
> The first form of poverty is poverty of spirit. The nature of this poverty of spirit is not understood by the common people. If a soul that possesses this poverty of

[7] John 1:1.

> spirit abounds even with all the treasures of this world, it considers them as mere passing trinkets. Such a soul flies to Heaven without the aid of wings! Such souls can drink from the font of celestial joy while they still live in their mortal lives, for they are spiritually united to God. They graze in the pastures of Heaven even as they make their way there. They long for nothing that can be seen with the physical eyes, or anything that can be understood by the human mind, or anything that is known and valued by the common multitude of people.
>
> The second form of poverty dismisses all things of this world completely. It strips itself of everything and gives away all that it possesses, completely submitting itself to the yoke of holy obedience. It lives in faith, hope, and charity and is firmly grounded in the fear of God. Therefore, it is also able to drink from the font of heavenly joys.
>
> The third form of poverty takes all its delight in the love of God and cares nothing for the anxieties of this passing world in which it is situated. Rather, it clings only to the supreme and highest Good. It gladly and unreservedly offers itself as a gift to this supreme Goodness, even while in this life. Whatever happens to it, good or bad, it rejoices and gives thanks. It lives as if in a peaceful and serene dream, obeying Christ completely in all things. Such a soul acquires a pure heart, and drinks from the heavenly font in peace and security.

At this point, the vision of St. Frances reached its end, and her soul was saddened by this. But then she heard a voice say to her:

> O soul, do not wish to be told anything more just now! Leave God to do His works, and when as He chooses, for

He does all things well and wisely. He is able to satisfy every soul who wishes it. Do not seek to fathom His reasons or to comprehend His ways, for He has determined all these before you even existed. He has promised you His love—let this suffice to you, for He is able to provide you with all you could ever need or desire.

Be content for now with a good and ready will, and unite yourself to Him without reservation. For His love is so great that it will fulfill all that you dream of and all that you hope for.

This vision occurred in the year of Our Lord 1432, in the month of February.

Vision 8

February 13, 1432

On another occasion, after receiving the Most Holy Sacrament of the Body of Christ in the same Chapel of the Holy Angels, St. Frances, the servant of Christ, devoted herself to prayer and meditation, as was her custom. During this time, she experienced her spirit's being taken up into an immense light, while her body remained within the chapel.

After she had returned to her usual senses, her spiritual father, Canon Matteotti, questioned her about what she had experienced and witnessed during that time. Under holy obedience, she related how she had perceived a most beautiful and radiant light, from which shone forth many and splendid flashes and beams of brightness. But under this great light, there was a very thick and dense darkness.

Within the heart of the vast light St. Frances perceived a blazing fire of the most extreme brilliance, and upon this fire, there was positioned a tabernacle of incredible beauty and ornateness. On top of this beautiful and precious tabernacle, there was enthroned our glorious Savior. He was visible to Frances in His most sacred humanity. His essence glowed with a multitude of indescribable splendors, which the human eye could barely look upon or comprehend.

Yet the form of His holy humanity remained perfectly clear through the radiant brilliance that surrounded and emanated from Him. His sacred wounds were visible upon His human form, and incandescent, flaming rays beamed forth out of them. There was a multitude of souls of the blessed arrayed around Him, and these rays illuminated them in a miraculous fashion so that they, too, became glowing.

There were indeed a great many souls assembled there, in a crowd that surpassed number. The Queen of Heaven was there also in the primary place of honor, wearing upon her head a triple crown. It was from the great and immaculate Mother of God, among all the inhabitants of Heaven, that the brightest and most intense light shone forth.

Frances noticed other souls there as well who were still united with their mortal bodies. These entered and exited freely from the blazing fire within the vast light, without harm or impediment. Frances knew in her heart that this fire was nothing other than the flame of divine love. Hence, she earnestly desired to learn who were these souls who were capable of freely entering and exiting this mystical fire. And it was revealed to her that these were the souls of living human beings who persevered faithfully in the love of God and who came regularly to renew and refresh themselves with this sacred flame.

As the saint stood staring intently and joyously at this wondrous sight, St. Mary Magdalene, the ardent lover of Christ, together with the virgin martyr St. Agnes, approached her. They persuaded Frances that she should venture with them to approach the fire more closely. And they directed her vision to some of the other things that were present within that realm of the blessed.

First, they pointed out to Frances a great troupe of the holy virgin saints, each of whom wore upon her head a resplendent golden tiara, embellished with precious jewels. St. Mary Magdalene then commenced a graceful and perfectly ordered dance, which the other virgin saints joined. Frances was amazed to see them all singing and dancing in perfect harmony, as they entered and exited freely the flame of divine love!

In tuneful chorus, they sang thus:

If any wish to be Christ's bride,
Let them spurn all useless pride,
Put aside each earthly thing,
Seeking nothing but their King!
Let them do His will alone,
Gazing on His holy throne;
To their Lord all things they give;
For Him only do they live.
To their God they ever lift
Minds and hearts and souls as gift!
From the Lord's own grace so free,
The gifts they offer now are three.
First, they keep within their minds
Thoughts of Jesus' love divine,
Always seeking to fulfill
God's most wise and holy will.
Next, they give their very hearts
To the God who love imparts,
Trusting all their cares to Him,
Fearing nothing but to sin.

Third, they offer God their soul,
Trusting His most wise control,
Seeking never their own praise,
To the Lord their souls they raise!

While St. Frances had still been in her state of trance, she had sung these very words aloud and even made the dancing motions of the choir of holy virgins. All this was witnessed by her spiritual father, Canon Matteotti, and corresponded perfectly to the narration of her vision that Frances had made afterward.

Next, she had heard St. Mary Magdalene singing on her own, addressing her words to the Holy Mother of God.

> Praise to you, O Queen of Heaven [she sang], who are adorned with all virtues and were greeted by the angel of the Lord as being full of grace! Through your humility and divine piety, you have liberated us from our ruin. In your virginial womb you received the Word of God and clothed Him with your own flesh. Hence, Christ was born of you as both God and man. He it is who has rescued us from death and freed us from the chains of mortality. To you be infinite praise, O Empress of the Angels, adorned, raised up, and crowned as Queen by your own Son! You are our light and our joy in this blessed life.

Then St. Catherine of Alexandria,[8] a virgin martyr and a royal bride of Christ, broke also out into song. With great exultation, she acclaimed:

[8] St. Catherine of Alexandria was a virgin martyr who lived in Alexandria in Egypt in the fourth century. She was widely venerated as an intercessor and example of female sanctity in Europe in the late Middle Ages.

We all delight with heart and voice,
And as one chorus we rejoice
That this Kingdom now is ours,
And Christ our everlasting Spouse!

This vision occurred in the year of Our Lord 1432, on the thirteenth day of February.

Vision 9

March 31, 1432

At another time, after receiving the Most Holy Sacrament of the Body of Christ in the aforementioned Chapel of the Holy Angels in the Basilica of Santa Maria in Trastevere, St. Frances, the servant of God, was taken up into a spiritual ecstasy. After she had returned to her natural senses, her spiritual father, Canon Matteotti, questioned her carefully about her experiences and what she had seen and witnessed. Under holy obedience, the saint proceeded to relate to him how she had been raised up in spirit into the highest sphere of the Heavens. She found herself led into the presence of the angelic choir of the seraphim, but only within the lowest section of that highest choir of the angels.

There she experienced an intense but most sweet and delightful warmth radiating forth. The delightful warmth inflamed all of the angelic host, both in the choir of the seraphim and also those in the lower ranks. The spirit of St. Frances, the handmaid of Christ, was also delightfully inflamed by this comforting celestial warmth.

As the saint gazed upon the throne of the Divinity, one of the angels of the seraphic choir spoke to her. He said:

> This is the highest Deity, whose splendor and charity inflame us all! We all rejoice in the warmth and radiance of His love. O blessed, soul, take care that you persevere

in your holy intentions, for He who is Love Itself is awaiting you and wishes you to overcome yourself for His sake.

Let your heart be ever pure and innocent, and keep your intention toward almighty God always reverent and righteous. Strive to ascend ever higher the mountain of divine love! And abide in devout contemplation of the divine love, which thus inflames and transforms you. For the soul that is united to love is indeed transformed by it! It is elevated, just as you have been, above the very heavens, and is led into the company of the choir of the seraphim.

Yes, the warmth of divine love inflames the heart inebriated with it; it warms and it inflames, yet it does not incinerate or burn. One who experiences this is no longer conscious of himself or aware of his own selfhood.

But it is divine charity alone that allows such a soul to sustain this great love. This love is a deep abyss that is not able to be fathomed or comprehended. The spirit that once enters into it is no longer able to be satisfied with the passing world only, which is dark and scattered with thorns. Rather, it longs fervently and constantly for the beautiful and heavenly love that gives it healing of its pains and bliss beyond all imagining!

This was in the year of Our Lord 1432, on the final day of the month of March.

Vision 10

April 3, 1432

Another time, after St. Frances had received the Most Holy Sacrament in the same chapel as before, she entered into a state of mystical ecstasy for a time. After she had returned to her normal consciousness, her spiritual father, Canon Matteotti, asked her to relate to him all that she had witnessed and experienced while in a state of trance.

She then told him how her soul had been led up into an immensely bright light. Within that light, she beheld the Queen of Heaven, seated upon a golden throne of wondrous beauty. Underneath the throne was a glowing fire. And Frances somehow knew this fire to be nothing other than divine love.

She then heard a voice proceeding from the flames and addressing her. It said:

> O blessed soul, have your heart made ready for the celestial blessings that have been especially prepared for you! Diligently commit to your memory all the things that are revealed to you, and order your mind and heart carefully, so that you may become perfect in virtue and piety. For your beloved divine Spouse, Our Lord Jesus Christ, is coming soon, and if He finds you thus prepared and awaiting Him, He will choose you as His own!

Your love of Him will make you tranquil and content. Unite yourself to this love, and you shall then be transformed through the eternal and supreme blessings and beauties that are pleasing to Him. Having been enriched by His gifts, hold firmly to that which has been granted you. And do not doubt that you will receive even fuller graces from Him, when and how it pleases Him to bestow them upon you.

Exult in this love, and unite yourself to the abyss of love and ardor. For this alone will lead you to know more perfectly your most sweet and beloved Spouse, who is the perfection of love. He will grant you strength and will adorn you with a treasury of interior graces. These graces shall not be seen by the world. Yes, though these graces of love cannot be perceived from the outside, they will illuminate your inner being with infinite splendor. They will strengthen and inflame your heart and will clothe and adorn you with the most perfect beauty!

So stand ready and wait, O blessed soul, for the time when He will call you. Keep your mind quiet and tranquil, and be content with whatever He wills for you at the present time. Do not involve yourself in affairs that do not concern you, but be diligently attentive to the purity of your own interior life.

This vision took place in 1432, on the third day of April.

Vision 11

April 22, 1432

Another time when St. Frances, the handmaid of Christ, had received the Most Holy Sacrament in the aforementioned chapel, as she prayed and meditated after her reception of the holy Body of the Lord, she entered into a state of deep trance.

Her spirit was then led from a certain brilliant light into another place, which was incredibly high and glorious. She related all this to her spiritual father, Canon Matteotti, under the bonds of holy obedience. From there, the glorious Evangelist St. John took her spirit into the presence of God's eternal glory. In this blazing and refulgent glory, she perceived the most holy humanity of the Savior in dazzling triumph.

All the spiritual inhabitants of Heaven were also assembled there, both the angelic host and the souls of the blessed. Together these all gave praise to Christ with indescribable joy and exultation, thanking Him earnestly for the redemption of the human race from the dominion of sin and death.

As Blessed Frances gazed upon this marvelous sight, St. John the Evangelist spoke to her, saying:

> O soul, take care to be established in humility, and trust in these things that are revealed to you. For through these

visions, Divine Love shall come to you and draw you beyond yourself. Ensure that you are always unfailingly obedient and faithful in service, and do not let anything whatsoever impede you from this holy commitment. Cultivate true purity, which is spotless and clean, for this is pleasing to God.

Reflect upon the Highest Power, who is able to provide all good things to those who love Him. And consider carefully your own behavior toward this all-powerful God. No one should be impeded in his love of God by things that do not concern him. And, as far as matters that really *do* concern you, there is a sure and beautiful remedy for all distraction and anxiety in the holy fear of God, which liberates the soul from all other concerns and worries.

It is true obedience that makes the soul free and rescues it from the snares of the foe. It is obedience and humility that render the soul most beautiful and beloved in the sight of God. When these are fully cultivated and developed, the mind is purified, and the soul is freed from all blemishes and stains. It is transformed, and it transcends itself to enter into unity with God Himself. Strive to free yourself of all cares and concerns about yourself, for it is through this trusting self-abandonment to God that you shall be invited to the great feast of the Divine Word, united to humanity.

After this, the holy Evangelist St. John addressed his words directly to the Savior. He spoke thus: "O most high and almighty Lord, who are elevated above all the Heavens! You cause souls to depart from the flesh in due course, for it is not fitting that the immortal spirit should abide forever in the mortal flesh. Thus,

You liberate souls from the bonds of space and time and grant unto them the capacity of gazing upon Your own ineffable glory for all eternity!"

The blessed handmaid of Christ, St. Frances, made known to her spiritual father all that had been revealed to her in this vision, all that she had come to perceive as if by gazing through a sacred looking glass into the beauty and splendor of the Divinity.

This took place in 1432, on the twenty-second day of April.

Vision 12

April 1432

Once when Blessed Frances had entered into the same Chapel of the Holy Angels, so that, in accordance with the instructions of her spiritual father, she should receive Holy Communion while Mass was celebrated, she was taken up into ecstasy while the Mass was proceeding. While she was still in this mystical state, she received the Body of the Lord with profound reverence, showing great awe and wonder as she did so. Afterward, she returned to her normal consciousness.

Under obedience to her spiritual father, she described to him what she had experienced while she was in her state of trance during the Mass and the reception of the Blessed Sacrament. First, her spirit was taken up into a bright light, and from this place of brightness she was led by the glorious St. John the Baptist to an even higher and more radiant realm. He spoke to her, saying: "Stand here, O soul, and you shall witness the wonderful, holy things that are to take place!"

Frances then saw a huge, splendid throne, gleaming with gold and adorned with magnificent jewels, in which the Savior Himself was nobly seated. She knew that He was fully present there in both His most holy humanity and His divine majesty. And from the divine majesty of the Savior there radiated forth an indescribable splendor. This refulgent splendor was of such dazzling intensity that Frances could perceive nothing at all in this unearthly brilliance except for His sacred human form.

St. Frances witnessed also the Queen of Heaven, the crowned Mother of the Son of God, who was present as well. She was showing reverence and honor to her divine Child, who was seated in glory upon His supreme throne. There were also the apostles, patriarchs, prophets, and martyrs, together with the holy virgins, confessors, and a multitude of other saints.

In fact, all the angelic and human spirits of the blessed who dwell in Heaven were there, all arranged in fitting order. They were singing together exultant praise to Jesus Christ, the Son of God, in waves of undulating, celestial harmony. Their ineffable canticle expressed, above all, fervent gratitude for the mystery of His most holy Passion, which He underwent out of pure love to unite our human nature to the immortal spirits of the blessed. All of these angels and saints in Heaven were illuminated and inflamed by the brilliant splendor that shone forth from Christ upon His throne.

And then the glorious St. John the Baptist appeared and spoke to St. Frances. He said:

> Prepare yourself well to receive Love, who has invited you to His solemn banquet! Diligently keep yourself as clean and pure as possible, and endeavor to remove all stain of sin and vice from your heart, so that you may shine for Him. Yes, strive, O blessed soul, to be properly and fittingly presented for the celestial banquet to which Your Spouse has summoned you. Trample under your feet all memories of and desires for the things of the passing world! Remove from yourself all that is harmful, and cling to what is truly good alone.

> Enlighten your mind, so that in what you see you may comprehend the glory and love of God, which surpass all imagining. Strengthen your resolve firmly in love. You will find, O soul, tranquility and firmness within a certain precious gemstone—this precious gemstone is, in fact, the pearl of *humility*, adorned with holy *obedience*.
>
> Come confidently and joyfully to the heavenly feast of Holy Communion, and you shall hear there new songs. Yes, there you will see beautiful and wondrous things such as you have never imagined—miraculous and marvelous things, indeed, that even when seen can scarcely be comprehended!

Frances saw other angelic spirits there who were carefully and reverently preparing an altar. Then the celestial King, whom she had seen earlier seated upon the glorious throne of majesty, took on the form of a radiant angel Himself. In this form, He positioned Himself over the altar. Yet somehow (in a way that Frances could not fully understand or describe), He also remained simultaneously enthroned in glory as He was before.

And so it was that the handmaid of God, St. Frances, saw the majesty of the wondrous King seated upon His splendid throne and also saw Him positioned above the altar, in an angelic form. From the head, hands, feet, and side of the latter angelic form there flowed forth an abundance of a most precious substance in great streams, as if from an inexhaustible source.

And she noticed the apostles sitting in reverent attendance around this altar. Then they all suddenly arose and approached the altar. St. Peter took his position, as if he was the priest at a Mass. From the precious substance that had flowed forth from the angelic form of Christ over the altar, he ministered to the multitude of angels and souls of the blessed there present. The other apostles also dutifully assisted him in this task.

When all this had occurred, the glorious Baptist again appeared before the devout soul of St. Frances. Approaching her, he led her forth by the hand to the altar. There St. Peter showed to her the angelic form above the altar, indicating it to her with the utmost reverence and awe. He also invited her to touch the sacred head of Christ in this angelic form. As St. Peter and Frances both gazed in love and wonder upon its ineffable beauty, the Prince of the Apostles said to her:

> Behold, O blessed and chosen soul, the noble head and the precious mouth of Him who, in His mercy and love, made Himself visible for wretched souls sunken in sin and misery! He submitted Himself to God the Father in perfect obedience and thereby poured forth an abundant river of graces, from which those who were sorely parched with bitter thirst might drink freely and deeply and be wonderfully refreshed.
>
> Behold, O holy soul, His innocent and pure hands, which pour forth this inexhaustible river of heavenly grace, whose sparkling waters nourish and refresh the souls of those who love and fear the Lord. It was He Himself, with these very hands, who created and fashioned the human race, and in His love, redeemed and perfected them.
>
> Behold His feet—the feet of Him who was so eager to redeem the human race that He proceeded from the Heavens, uttering no word but drawn by the purest love. Yes, He went forth unhesitatingly as a speedy arrow rushing to our aid, even to the point of sustaining all the punishments

due for our sins and enduring a grim and agonizing death itself, thereby conquering our final enemy.

O most devout soul, look upon His chest, pierced and inflamed with the fervor of His love! So great and so compelling was this love that He willingly bore all our punishments and our sins and sorrows. For this sacred chest of Christ pours out an endless stream of ardor, which enters into souls who are united with Him through love.

Behold, finally, His complete form, which was and is so kindly and compassionate. Follow His example, even though you should not believe for an instant that your own merits make you qualified or capable of doing so. For He Himself is truly the Kingdom of Heaven, in which the one who wishes to reign gives himself fully for the sake of love. And it behooves anyone who aspires to live and reign in glory with Him to strip himself of all other attachments and all extraneous distractions and desires!

Then St. Peter once more approached the holy altar with great reverence and carefully took a particle from the most precious substance that had flowed forth from Christ in His angelic form. This particle he placed into the mouth of Blessed Frances, while she was still in her state of ecstasy. While this was happening, her spiritual father, Canon Matteotti (who was a witness to the whole scene), had seen Frances visibly open her mouth to receive something into it, while she was still in a state of trance.[9]

After placing this precious particle in her mouth, St. Peter, the Prince of the Apostles, spoke thus to the saint:

9 Presumably this coincided with her reception of the Eucharist in the Mass.

> It is divine love which, in its power and strength, renders a soul stable and firm! In a secret and mysterious manner, it inflames the soul, while it knows it not, and transforms it into its own image and likeness. It nourishes and satisfies it with the very bread of Heaven, and makes it become utterly inebriated with love. The Most High King of the Heavens thus creates the soul anew, lovingly refashioning it into something unspeakably and incomprehensibly wonderful, by virtue of His own infinite strength and power!

St. Frances remained in her state of ecstasy during the Mass, including when she received Holy Communion. Her spiritual father, Canon Matteotti, sensed a fragrance of remarkable sweetness at this time, as if the entire chapel were filled with a multitude of roses and other flowers. And it was not only her spiritual father who noticed this, but several of Frances's spiritual daughters who were present distinctly perceived the scent as well. This sweet and heavenly fragrance occurred not only on this occasion but also in many other instances when Frances was taken into ecstasy.

This vision occurred in April, in the year of Our Lord 1432.

Vision 13

Easter Sunday 1432

At another time, after St. Frances had received the Most Holy Sacrament of the Body of Christ in the aforementioned Chapel of the Holy Angels in the Basilica of Santa Maria in Trastevere in Rome, she entered into a state of mystical ecstasy while she was engaged in prayer and meditation. When this happened, her whole body became perfectly immobile. But after a time, while she remained in a trance, Frances began to move once more and sang most sweetly the praises of God and His Virgin Mother, showing forth signs of marvelous happiness and joy.

She then returned to her normal senses and consciousness. At this point, her spiritual father, Canon Matteotti, questioned her concerning what she had witnessed and experienced while in her state of ecstasy or trance. St. Frances told him that her spirit had been led upward, moving from a certain bright light to an extremely high place. In this very high place, she was able to gaze upon the souls of the blessed in all their celestial glory and splendor. And although she could not mingle in the company of these blessed spirits (which included saints and holy angels), nevertheless she was there in the place where they dwelt, as if in a special section reserved for guests and visitors.

The soul of St. Mary Magdalene, to whom Frances had a particular devotion, then approached her. St. Mary Magdalene was, of course, a saint filled with a love of Christ that was fervent and passionate beyond all others. This loving disciple of Christ then spoke to Frances, saying:

> Allow yourself to be completely captured by love, O devout soul! All these things that you now see, you are able to perceive only because of the intense love for you of Him who is Himself an abyss of infinite love. Therefore, be attentive to all that you see and sense here.
>
> Truly, there is no one who is capable of sustaining the immensity of the power that has drawn you here and that now supports you. Nor is there anyone who could comprehend the eternal wisdom that has created you and determined your destiny and has now led you, as a guest and a pilgrim, into this realm of eternal joy.
>
> O faithful soul, give sincere thanks to this Divine Love, who has led you into this celestial and glorious realm! It is this Love Itself that has brought you here and has made you beautiful by Its grace. Taste deeply of this rich sweetness! Contemplate it with a mind made pure, always grounded in earnest humility.
>
> While you remain in the mortal flesh, you shall be subject to the sufferings and pains that are an inescapable part of earthly life. But when you pass from your earthly life, these shall be able to touch you no more. Therefore, be strong in the face of all adversities, knowing that they shall not last for long, and then you will obtain for yourself unending honor.

After this, St. Frances beheld the glorified humanity of Jesus Christ, Our Savior. It was bathed in a dazzling and astonishing brilliance that surpassed all imagining and comprehension. So intense was this brightness that it was as if she could perceive nothing at all clearly or distinctly, except for a certain human form.

Next, she saw the Mother of the Son of God, looking more radiant and beautiful than ever. This was because of her joy at the Resurrection of her Son, which was on that day being especially celebrated in Heaven as well, just as it was being celebrated on earth on that particular day.[10] All the glorious spirits of the angels and the souls of the blessed then venerated the Mother of God with the greatest honor, giving her thanks for being found uniquely worthy to carry Christ in her sacred, virginal womb. They praised her also for the indescribable love she felt for the King of Heaven, which led her to endure the greatest of agonies while her Son suffered on the Cross.

Among those paying their homage to the Blessed Virgin were the holy apostles. Next came St. Mary Magdalene, filled with the most fervent love for the Lord Jesus, and then the entire choir of blessed virgin saints. These sang to Mary:

> Praise to you, O high Queen, because of your blessed poverty, which has exalted us all and raised us to a place of glory. O Mary, immaculate Mother, you are full of every grace that God can bestow!
>
> And thanks also to You, O sweetest Father, who gave Your very own Son for our salvation. And thanks to You, immortal Son, for it was Your immense humility that won for us this Kingdom! And You made Your blessed

[10] This vision occurred on Easter Sunday. This suggests that while the Solemnity of the Resurrection of the Lord was being celebrated with particular joy on earth, its joy was reflected also in Heaven.

> Mother a sharer in Your reign, for she is now Queen of the Heavens, raised above all creation and all the choirs of angels. And in this exalted place of majesty, she beholds, directly and fully, You, O Christ, and the eternal Father in all Your ineffable glory!
>
> Let boundless praise be forever given unto You, O Son of the Divine Majesty; and to you, O Virgin and Mother, be infinite grace and gratitude. Through Your fullness of truth, O Christ, we have salvation. Together with You, we rejoice in the nobility of such a sweet and wondrous Mother. You have glorified Your Mother, and in Your humility You console and comfort us.
>
> O blessed Mary, God the Father, in His eternal divinity, has chosen you as His daughter; and the Son, in His most holy humanity, has chosen you as His Mother; while the Holy Spirit has chosen you as His beloved and eternal spouse. O high Queen of Heaven and Empress of the Angels, you are the true comfort and solace of all human souls, and no less are you the joy of those who dwell in Heaven!

While St. Frances was in this state of ecstatic trance, she was directed to join her voice with the song of praise of the blessed spirits. This she did, and so all of those present heard her sing the words of praise that are recorded above. She did this while still in a state of trance.

Then St. Mary Magdalene spoke to St. Frances. "Be comforted, O happy soul," she said, "and be grateful for all that has been revealed to you this day. Give thanks to the Lord, who has permitted you to perceive this vision of the magnitude of His love."

At this point, St. Frances sensed that her vision was about to draw to its close. She was deeply saddened at the thought of having to depart, and she burst into bitter tears. Then St. Mary Magdalene reproved her for this, saying, "Do not weep, my child!"

But St. Francis responded thus to St. Mary Magdalene: "You yourself were reduced to weeping and mourning when you were separated for the Lord for only a short time, and you then sustained such pains as I now feel. Therefore, do not be surprised if you see me weep now, since I know that this wonderful vision must end soon, and during my ordinary, waking life I remain at a distance from Christ and cannot see Him constantly."

This vision happened in 1432, on the day of the solemnity of the Resurrection of the Lord.

Vision 14

May 1, 1432

After reception of the Most Precious Sacrament once again in the aforementioned Chapel of the Holy Angels, Blessed Frances remain perfectly still for a time in prayer and meditation. While she was engrossed in this prayer and meditation, she entered into a state of trance and experienced a vision. When she had returned to her usual senses, her spiritual father, Canon Matteotti, questioned her, under the bonds of spiritual obedience, about what she had perceived during the time when she had departed from waking consciousness.

Frances related to him how the spirit of David, the king and prophet, had led her forth to witness a certain divine revelation. He spoke to her thus:

> Come, O soul, and make no delay! For your heavenly Spouse awaits you at His celestial table. There, He will transform you and render you capable of looking up His blessed glory and divine essence.
>
> Consider the company that shall be gathered at this glorious banquet—the holy angels and the souls of all the saints. If you contemplate this celestial society, you will surely not fail to be captured by ardent love and longing. For they enjoy the utter perfection of blessings

> continuously and without cessation, and all are completely saturated with love for Him who gave Himself for us. Such indeed is very clear!
>
> Therefore, urge yourself to love God fervently, and seek nothing beyond Him whom you love. May you constantly stand firm, O soul. Contemplate this heavenly banquet in which God Himself will absorb you into His divine essence. For He assuredly burns with love for you, and this is why He welcomes your soul to this celestial table.
>
> O devout soul, do not treat this as if it were a little thing, nor be sluggish and slothful in accepting God's invitation. And do not allow yourself to become entangled in the passing cares and allurements of the earth, for these may very easily become an impediment to you. Allow yourself to be inflamed with the love of God, and let this be your strength and your comfort. Let others say what they will, but *you* must never abandon the Lord Jesus Christ.

Then the blessed soul of St. Frances saw suddenly the glorified humanity of Jesus the Savior—that is, His humanity united with His divinity. But this wonderful vision lasted only momentarily, even though the saint remained in her state of mystical trance. And she felt greatly grieved that it had ended so quickly.

When the vision of the glorified humanity of Christ ended, the prophet David approached her once again, accompanied by two angels. He bore at his chest a certain most beautiful musical instrument, resembling a ten-stringed lyre. This he played in wondrous fashion with unfathomable artistry and skill, all the while singing the psalms in a voice of incredible sweetness. To Blessed Frances, the sound of the voice seemed to dominate the instrument, and the sound of these vocal melodies was so exalted and intricate in its harmony that it seemed to her impossible that they should be produced by the single voice of the prophet David alone.

While remaining in her state of trance, St. Frances spoke to David, expressing her sadness that he had apparently caused her vision of the glorified Christ to end. "Oh, with these songs of yours, beautiful as they are," she said, "you have removed me from the most blessed vision in which I was able to gaze upon the supreme goodness of Christ's glory!"

Now, St. Frances's spiritual father, Canon Matteotti, together with one of her spiritual daughters in Christ by the name of Rita, both clearly heard Frances speak these words while she was in her state of mystical trance.

This vision took place in the year of Our Lord 1432, on the first day of the month of May.

Vision 15

May 10, 1432

In another instance, when St. Frances, the handmaid of God, had received the Sacrament of the Body of Christ in the Chapel of the Holy Angels already often mentioned, her body was rendered perfectly immobile. She then experienced her blessed spirit's being led up into a great, holy light and from there was taken into an even brighter and more stupendous light.

Here, the glorious Doctor of the Church St. Jerome appeared. He spoke to Frances, addressing her thus: "O noble soul, raise yourself up to enjoy the blessings of your Creator, who has given permission to me that I may reveal Him to you!"

Then the spirit of Frances suddenly witnessed an exalted and majestic throne, on which the Incarnate Word of God sat in all His incomparable glory. Because of the brilliance both of the throne and One who sat therein, Frances was utterly dazzled and could perceive nothing but a certain human form.

The spirit of Frances was positioned in a place separate (as if reserved for guests and passing pilgrims) from all the souls of the saints and the glorious angels who were there—for she was, in fact, in Heaven itself. She remained there for about an hour, filled with joy and wonder that surpassed all description.

As this time drew to an end, the holy Doctor St. Jerome addressed her once more. He said in a voice of great gravity:

> O soul, you are accustomed often to lament at your earthly pilgrimage and your separation from your heavenly homeland. And you often wish that things would happen in accordance with your own will and desires. But you are privileged to be permitted into the wonders and delights of the contemplation of the highest majesty of Christ, which you now see as if in a mirror and darkly. You believe that already you may have seen too much; but I tell you, you have really seen very little at all! Such is the unfathomable vastness and magnitude of the abyss of pure contemplation of the highest and omnipotent Lord.
>
> Even we blessed spirits who stand within the assembly of saints do not see absolutely everything of God's glory. Much less it is that you now perceive, for you are here only as a guest and pilgrim, and gaze in as if through a window!
>
> O Frances, you are blessed and fortunate to have a heart that is innocent and pure, in this respect, as white as the snow; you are blessed, too, to have a mind that is passionately inflamed with divine love, and which thus glows with the red of the ardent rose. It is a truly beautiful thing to combine these two colors—the white of innocence and the crimson of love! Take care that you maintain this double blessing carefully and diligently in the face of all the trials of the world. For if you preserve this rare and privileged treasure, you will certainly ascend to this place of glory. Indeed, it is your combination of innocence and love that now permits you to behold the vision that you

> see. Take comfort and strength in this fact. And now, Frances, you must return to your normal life!

At this point, Frances resumed her mobility, although she remained in a state of trance. And she argued with St. Jerome, protesting against being sent away from the glorious place to which her spirit had been taken during her vision. Her spiritual father, Canon Matteotti, and the aforementioned Rita both heard this clearly.

But then the great Doctor of the Church reprimanded Frances:

> O soul, you are not being humble now in presuming that it is possible for you to stay here at this time! Rather, you are being very audacious and bold. You do not fully comprehend where you are, nor the vastness of the abyss of contemplation which is here. For now, simply be strong in your love of God, and be ready to continue your earthly pilgrimage for just as long as God wishes it.
>
> You often imagine that you are perfectly obedient. Yet if you were really perfectly obedient and had overcome your self-will completely, you would accept what I say with complete submission, for I speak as God directs me. If it pleases God and the court of Heaven for you now to leave this vision and to return to your normal life, then you ought to obey without protest. What is true denial of self, except a readiness to deny oneself those experiences that bring the greatest delight? Why are you not content to do this, but instead you argue with me? It is the spiritual joy and pleasure that you do not wish to be parted from—you still wish things to happen in accordance with your own will and preferences!
>
> But a soul that resigns itself entirely to the will of God and is prepared to lose even spiritual joys and consolation

in accordance with His will is truly obedient. Through such obedience, it will remain tranquil and content in whatever conditions it finds itself. Be content and accepting in all things, and then alone will you know yourself to be truly obedient to the will of God. But the soul that devotes itself to prayer and experiences the joys of divine contemplation and then becomes dejected and discouraged if it loses them is not truly obedient. Such a soul mistakenly imagines that it is no longer united with God, and many such people throw themselves into rivers or commit other acts of despair.

But the soul that is invariably content and tranquil and experiences the joys of divine contemplation remains equally content and tranquil when these joys come to an end. This withdrawal of the joys of contemplation is a form of testing and purification by God. These souls can encounter anything in life, either trials or temptations, and they are able to withstand them confidently. For nothing can separate them from the love of God.

St. Frances experienced this vision on the tenth day of May in the year of Our Lord 1432.

Vision 16

Solemnity of the Ascension 1432

Once more, after St. Frances, the servant of God, had received the Most Holy Sacrament in the same Chapel of the Holy Angels previously mentioned, she remained (as was her custom) in prayer and meditation on the great mystery in which she had partaken. During this time of prayer, she became completely still and entered into a state of mystical rapture, leaving her normal consciousness behind, as often happened to her. While in this state of trance, an angel appeared to her and led her spirit into a certain realm of bright light. From there, she was led to an even brighter and more radiant location, and there perceived a cloud of indescribably intense and refulgent splendor.

Within this, there was the ever-glorious Queen of Heaven, surrounded by wonderful and beautiful spirits who were doing her homage and singing her praises with the greatest of joy. But the eyes of the Blessed Mother of God were turned upward, for there was above her a vision of her divine Son ascending into His glory.

Mary then spoke to Frances, saying:

> O most fortunate spirit who have come here, arise and look upward to see the ascension of my Son, so that your

heart may be deeply captured by love of Him! Behold the supreme Redeemer of the universe, who has ascended above all the Heavens. It is He who has opened the Kingdom of Heaven to us all! And it is He who has made the souls of the blessed to become citizens of the celestial and eternal city, the new Jerusalem, in which we are all constantly in perfect union and peace.

Consider the infinite and unimaginable heights He has attained through His wondrous Ascension! He goes up in splendid triumph as the true and invincible Savior of the world, and He carries His noble flag of victory with Him. And once He has attained to the supercelestial heights, He does honor to His unseen Father, who is the source of all that exists.

These words were expressed by the Blessed Virgin in tones so sweet and mellifluous that it surpassed the purest and most refined of earthly music. And as Frances heard them, she experienced herself being drawn upwards in the illuminated vastness into which Christ Himself had just ascended!

There she found herself positioned, as a guest and pilgrim, among the choir of the seraphim. Gazing toward the highest point above her, she found that her vision was completely overcome by the surpassing brightness. Through this overwhelming blaze of refulgence, all she could make out was a certain human form, which she knew was the humanity of Jesus Christ.

Then there began something that resembled a very solemn and grand liturgical celebration. The choir of the seraphim began to sing, as if responding to the Queen of Heaven. Their song ran thus:

O praise to Thee, Jesus,
Who opens the door
To Heaven's bright Kingdom,
To reign evermore!
To angels most holy,
To saints ever blest,
Is granted a Kingdom
Of bliss and of rest.

Then the Queen of Heaven turned her eyes of infinite mercy once more to St. Frances, and she spoke thus: "O blessed soul, you are especially privileged to have been granted a vision of this most exalted and glorious majesty, which very few mortals have ever witnessed or even imagined!"

Next, the venerable company of the holy patriarchs approached the Blessed Virgin, showing great reverence and humility. Like the angels, they broke out into a joyous chant, singing:

O Empress of Heaven,
All thanks be to thee.
The Fruit whom thy womb bore
Has set our souls free!

Despite this chant in her honor, the attention of Blessed Mary remained completely fixed upon the divine heights to which her beloved Son had ascended. In tones of unbelievable beauty, she then sang:

Give thanks to the Father;
The Son now adore;
He's given you Heaven,
Thrown open its door!

Oh, here there's no sorrow,
Or sadness, or woe;
Eternal the gladness
The dwellers here know!

This wonderful vision took place in 1432, on the solemnity of the Lord's Ascension.

Vision 17

Solemnity of the Most Holy Trinity 1432

At another time, after reception of the Most Holy Sacrament in the same Chapel of the Holy Angels, the handmaid of Christ St. Frances applied herself assiduously to silent prayer and meditation upon the great mystery in which she had partaken. While engaged in these devotions, she entered into a state of mystical ecstasy or trance. In this state, she witnessed the solemn festivities that took place that day in Heaven, for it was then the great feast of the Most Holy Trinity. All the spirits in Heaven, both those of the holy angels and the souls of the blessed, partook in the awesome celestial liturgy that St. Frances was privileged to see.

When questioned by her spiritual father, Canon Matteotti, about what she had witnessed while in the state of trance, St. Frances had told him under obedience that she had heard a certain voice speaking to her. It said:

> O soul, may peace be with you always. Follow the truth of the Divine Love that has revealed these wonders and glories to you. Follow the Lord Jesus Christ, who is completely filled with love for you and feels the most abundant charity toward you.

Remain firmly and inseparably attached to Him in sincere love, and refuse ever to recede or depart from Him. And if you do that faithfully, you shall never lose your peace or tranquility, for it is indeed His divine will that you find your consolation in Him alone. Humble yourself before Him, and commit yourself unreservedly to His loving, compassionate heart. He will grant unto you the secret keys of that most Sacred Heart, and you shall always delight therein!

It is the virtue of pure and simple obedience that will unite you with Him most effectively, so be prompt to engage the virtue of obedience in every possible situation, almost before you sense it being asked of you. Permit yourself to be transformed in the Most Blessed Trinity, for it is God's power that has permitted you to look upon this vision. This is the sweet divine love that is also God's eternal wisdom and heavenly mercy. It is this divine love that will totally inflame and illumine your heart, if you permit it to do so.

O blessed soul, you already possess great depths. Turn your gaze unwaveringly to the great mystery of the highest Divinity, and contemplate it profoundly and reverently. Draw comfort and strength from this contemplation, O soul! For you shall, in due course, return to this place of glory and beauty if you remain steadfast in your love and abide always in unbreakable union with God.

Therefore, my child, cultivate this union with God most earnestly, and entrust yourself to Him entirely. You will not be anxious about any worldly matters or concerns as long as you stand firm in virtue and purity of conscience.

But, poor soul, how much pain you will sense when this vision ends and when you leave this celestial festival to return to your waking state! But govern yourself well and do not be discouraged or dejected; return to the table of the Blessed Eucharist in all your trials, and you shall find sure strength and sustenance there!

This vision occurred in the year of Our Lord 1432, on the solemnity of the Most Holy Trinity.

Vision 18

Solemnity of Corpus Christi 1432

Another time, St. Frances reverently received the Most Holy Sacrament in the same Chapel of the Holy Angels, and once again, she entered into a state of mystical trance while engaged in prayer. While in this condition, her body remained perfectly still. Afterward, she returned to her usual senses.

Her spiritual father, Canon Matteotti, then questioned her about what she had experienced and witnessed while in her state of trance, and she answered him under the bonds of holy obedience. She related how her spirit was first taken up into a certain light. From there, it was taken into another and even brighter light. Then, in turn, she was taken to yet a third light. This light was again more radiant and vaster than the previous one.

Within this light, she saw a certain table of incredible beauty that seemed to be aglow with an aura of holy love. Assembled around this table were many spiritual beings, whom Frances recognized to be the souls of the blessed. Upon the table, which was beautifully and ornately set, there was placed bread and wine, or at least what *appeared* to be bread and wine. For, through a certain mystical insight, the saint was able to perceive that the true substance of these was, in fact, Flesh and Blood.

Frances noticed that the various blessed souls assembled around the table derived great comfort, strength, and joy from the sight of the bread and the wine—but they, unlike her, did not perceive the hidden reality of the Flesh and the Blood that lay concealed under the appearances of the bread and the wine.

Frances related to her spiritual father that, although the blessed spirits assembled around the table were in close proximity to her, she was not permitted to mingle with them or to communicate with them. Rather, she was kept in a separate place, as if reserved for visitors and pilgrims. As she looked upon the beautiful table and the sacred banquet placed upon it, her heart was inflamed with an avid desire for this celestial nourishment and a profound devotion to God.

As she looked upon these precious treasures, suddenly the Queen of Heaven appeared before her. Holy Mary then addressed her thus:

> O devout soul, may you be well prepared for receiving the great gifts that await you in the future! It is the infinite love of God that has adorned you with these blessings. Keep this holy love always before the eyes of your mind, my child. Have your heart pure and open, in readiness for such a blessed and good gift, and be joyful in anticipating it.
>
> For what you see here is nothing less than the Incarnate Word of God, in His very flesh and blood, veiled under the appearances of bread and wine. This is the nourishment and food of all devout Christians, which sustains and supports them. Indeed, it is the delight of the holy angels and of the souls of the saints in Heaven, who dwell in the celestial city of God. All of these spirits who

partake of this banquet are filled with eternal illumination and unceasing joy.

God has given this vision to you now so that you may derive comfort, consolation, and strength from the great love that He feels toward you. This vision has been bestowed upon you so that you may truly know and appreciate the magnitude of the blessing you receive in the Most Holy Sacrament of the altar.

Meditate deeply on the magnitude of Divine Love, my daughter! How great is the humility of God, that He offers Himself to mere mortals under the appearances of bread and wine, so that you may partake even now in the wondrous delights of the Heavens! God gives Himself completely to you so that you all may be comforted in your sorrows and receive a foretaste of the eternal glory that awaits you.

Dispose yourself properly to enjoy the delight of the love offered to you, and strive to model yourself upon this great and unreserved love that you perceive here. Observe how eagerly Christ wishes to satisfy you out of His own plenitude and to give Himself fully to all who are able and willing to receive Him—those whose names have been inscribed in the Book of Life. O blessed soul, know that *your* name is written within that blessed Book of Life! Strive, therefore, to yield good, worthy fruit and always to grow in the love of God.

Be strong and firm always and maintain within your heart deep, sincere humility. In this way, you will be filled with bitterness whenever you see or encounter sin, which offends God and abounds in the world. Be prudent in your actions and perfect in your faith. Whenever you sense your faith to be weakening or some shade of sin to have stained your conscience, turn promptly to the Lord. Draw from Him and from His celestial love the mercy, consolation, and new strength that you need. Unite yourself continually to God in love, and He will render you agile and swift and will dispel all uncertainty and darkness from your heart.

When the holy Mother of God had concluded these words, St. Frances, the handmaid of Christ, spiritually communicated at this celestial table of her vision, receiving in this way the Precious Body and Blood of Jesus Christ.

Meanwhile, the whole multitude of the angelic host gazed upon the glory of God, and God, in turn, looked upon them with love. These blessed spirits were then filled with indescribable joy and commenced a hymn of unbelievable sweetness to the honor of the Most Holy Sacrament. And they said to Frances: "Rejoice, O Frances, and join in with our song!"

Now, Frances remained in her state of mystical trance, but at this point she commenced singing, just as she had been invited. She sang in a voice of incredible sweetness and was heard quite distinctly by both her spiritual father, Canon Matteotti, and her spiritual daughter, the aforementioned Rita. The song ran thus:

Let us thank the highest Lord,
Rightly by all saints adored!
He grants to us with Him to dine,
His Flesh the bread, His Blood the wine:
Banquet of supreme delight,
Flowing from great Heaven's height,
Prepared before the world began,
Heaven's bread bestowed on man.

Let us honor Christ our King,
His laud and glory ever sing.
With love He sets our hearts on fire,
Igniting there a pure desire!
To Mary, too, my thanks I give,
Whose grace and mercy help me live,
The Queen of angels and of earth,
Who gave to God Himself His birth!
All holy saints, I thank you, too,
For all you are and all you do,
For showing me your tender care
And hearing kindly all my prayers.
And Magdalene, my patron dear,
Thy burning passion quelled all fear,
My great example of true love,
My helper in the courts above.

At this point, the song came to an end, and St. Frances realized that her vision was also to conclude presently. Yet the angels and saints encouraged her still to continue her song of praise. But she responded with sorrow: "How can I continue with this joyful melody when my heart breaks within me? For I see that I must soon be separated from the glorious vision of holy love. It is for you, blessed saints and holy angels, who remain here that this song can continue. But as for me, who must return to the trials of earthly life, I must now cease to sing."

But still the angels and saints continued insistently to urge Frances to keep singing. So she complied with their request, finishing with a heartfelt prayer expressed in song. It ran thus:

O Love eternal and divine,
I'm weak and poor indeed,

Without Thine aid I'm all alone;
Thy help I ever need.
So grant me strength to win the fight—
My strength falls badly short;
Oh, teach my heart to cling to faith
And love Thee as I ought.

This vision took place in the year of Our Lord 1432, on the solemnity of Most Holy Body of Christ.

Vision 19

Solemnity of Sts. Peter and Paul, July 29, 1433

Another time, as she was praying and meditating following reception of the Most Holy Sacrament of the Body of Christ in the aforementioned Chapel of the Holy Angels in the Basilica of Santa Maria, the servant of God St. Frances was taken up into a spiritual ecstasy. While in this condition, she remained perfectly still in her body, but her spirit received a holy vision. In this vision, St. Benedict appeared to St. Frances and spoke with her, offering paternal instruction and encouragement. He said:

> O humble and poor soul, behold your own smallness, and consider the immensity in which God has deigned to place you! Seek not to remove yourself from where God has called you, nor seek to obtain more than what you have been granted by His infinite wisdom. For God shall be angered if you will for yourself more than He wills for you. Just imagine the heavenly city and the glories thereof, all of which await you. For its glory is the God of most beautiful love and light Himself! Let this be enough for you and be content and tranquil with the gifts that have been given you for now. And do whatever you judge to be a proper response to and a fitting employment of these same gifts.

O humble soul, why do you dare to be so bold that you desire to enter further than the wonderful place into which you have already been led? You stand already in a great abyss of love, yet you do not realize it. You are transformed by the Spirit, and already you look into a mirror of God. The graces and revelations you have been granted are such that many other devout souls envy you greatly! But remember that this grace is given to you and ordained by God alone, and not by your own merits.

Abide within yourself and be ever conscious of your own limitation and frailties. The more you humble yourself, the more honor you shall receive. Do not be pleased with yourself but be pleased rather with God, and be a good steward of the gifts that God has so generously bestowed upon you.

Oh, how vast are the gifts of God, for they are capable of making the soul do great things indeed! The more the soul is contented with holy poverty and simplicity, the more it will be saved through the Cross, which renders it free from all earthly attachment. Such a soul governs itself with assiduous care, and yet it is totally and passionately inflamed with divine love. And it finds its delight in the very One who has inflamed it with such wonderful and immense love.

O soul, love your Lord, and love Him perfectly! Love the gifts that He has given you. Make yourself heavenly and remove all earthbound affections from your heart. Strive to be wise when God opens your mind and imparts to you something of His eternal wisdom. For He is the abyss of love, who created you from nothing out of pure love. It is He who has made you also an instrument for the souls who follow you and are under your spiritual leadership. Tell these—that is, the sisters in your community—that the sister who leads herself to true devotion and finds quiet contentment in whatever God has ordained for her has truly managed herself well and admirably.

And know, Blessed Frances, that the glorious Mother is always interceding for you and is your advocate before almighty God. Assure your sisters that this is the case for each one of them!

This vision occurred in the year of Our Lord 1433, on the solemnity of Sts. Peter and Paul.

Vision 20

Christmas Day 1434

On another occasion, in the same chapel already often mentioned, St. Frances received the Most Holy Sacrament of the Body of Christ. As she prayed afterward, she was taken up into a mystical ecstasy or trance, and her body became immobile.

In this state, she had a vision of the Son of God while He was still a small infant, held in the arms of His Virgin Mother. Blessed Frances spoke to the Mother of God, begging her earnestly that she would let her hold her divine Son for a while. Frances's spiritual father, Canon Matteotti, and her spiritual daughter Rita both heard Frances make this request in tones of earnest entreaty while she was in her state of trance.

The Queen of Heaven then replied to Blessed Frances, saying: "O Frances, you would not be able to hold Him because of His immense weight! He is, after all, the Lord of the universe." But Frances responded to this by saying that, however heavy He might be, she still desired to hold Him. And so the Queen of the Angels gently placed her Son in the arms of the saint. And Frances, the handmaid of God, joyfully sang praises to God while lovingly holding the Son of God Himself in her arms.

The praises that St. Frances sang on the occasion have not been recorded by her spiritual father because of an illness he suffered at the time—but he does recall that they were truly wonderful.

This vision took place in the year 1434, on Christmas Day.

Vision 21

Feast of St. Stephen, December 26, 1439

Once, on a different Christmas Day, after St. Frances, the handmaid of God, had received the Holy Sacrament of the Body of Christ in the chapel of her own convent, she was taken up into ecstasy as she prayed. While she was in this state, she saw the Queen of Heaven tenderly cradling in her arms the Son of God. Frances was filled with deep longing to hold the Divine Infant, and she earnestly implored the Blessed Virgin that she should be permitted to do so.

To this, Mother Mary replied, "Not today, my daughter, not today! For on this solemnity, it is only I who enjoy the special privilege of holding my Son. But in a little while I shall permit you to cradle Him too." Having said this, Our Lady vanished, and St. Frances's vision came to an end.

The next day, which was the feast of St. Stephen, Frances, accompanied by several of her spiritual daughters, visited the Basilica of St. Lawrence (outside the walls of Rome) in order to venerate the body of St. Stephen, which is kept there. On the way back to their convent, they stopped at the Basilica of St. John Lateran to offer their devotions there too.

As Frances knelt before the major altar in that great basilica, she was again taken up into a mystical ecstasy, and she experienced the Son of God as an infant being placed into her arms by the Blessed Virgin. At once, she arose, still in a state of trance, and began to go to the Basilica of St. Mary Major, all the while holding the Infant Jesus in her arms (as it seemed to her in her vision)! She held her arms just as mothers are accustomed to do when cradling their babies, as all of her spiritual daughters clearly witnessed and attest. And although she was still in a state of trance, she walked with an assurance and confidence that was greater than if she had been in her natural senses.

When she entered the great Basilica of St. Mary Major, she remained there for a period of time. While still in a trance, she called upon a priest of the church and extended her arms, as if handing him an infant, and asked him to return the Holy Child to His Mother for her, with thanks for the special privilege granted to her.

After this, Frances made her way back to her own convent, accompanied by her spiritual daughters. All this time, she remained in a state of mystical ecstasy.

This took place in the year of Our Lord 1439, on the feast of St. Stephen.

VISION 22

Undated

On one occasion, after St. Frances, the beloved of God, had received the Sacrament of the Body of Christ in the Basilica of St. Cecilia in Trastevere, she entered into a state of trance. During this trance, which lasted about an hour, she remained perfectly still, not making the slightest movement.

After she returned to her natural senses, her spiritual father, Canon Matteotti, asked her to tell him if she had experienced or witnessed any blessed vision during the time when she had departed from her normal consciousness. So, under holy obedience, she related to him how she had looked upon the consecrated Host just before she received it. And it appeared to her to be transformed into a radiant, glowing flame.

At that point, she experienced her spirit's being drawn up into an extremely high place of incredible beauty and splendor. There she heard a resonant voice of ineffable and enchanting sweetness speaking to her. It said:

> Behold, I am the Divine Fire of love, who inflame the hearts of those who love Me! I set them aflame, yet I do not incinerate them. I lead those who love me to this refuge of peace and let them hear the celestial harmonies of the music of Heaven. The soul that, by the nobility of

its aspirations, is rendered capable of appreciating this glory and beauty desires to remain here forever and never to depart.

But I permit such a soul to remain here for only as long as I wish it to do so. I do this to fill the soul with desire and wonder at the greater and more exalted gifts that, in the fullness of time, I shall bestow upon all those who become truly pleasing to me!

Appendix

The Demonic Attacks Experienced by St. Frances of Rome

Recorded by Canon Giovanni Matteotti, her spiritual director

St. Frances experienced many dreadful and frightening attacks from demons throughout her life. Such demons, according to their accustomed practice, are apt to disguise themselves in a variety of forms, either to deceive or to frighten. They especially afflict those of the greatest sanctity, goaded on by envy and resentment of their devotion to God and in an attempt to discourage them or undermine their faith.

When St. Frances, the servant of God, first began to experience these attacks, the devil appeared to her disguised in the form of an old hermit. This hermit was clad in garments of incredible wretchedness and had a long, disheveled beard, and he held in his knotty hand a twisted wooden staff. But the handmaid of God instantly recognized him to be a demon in disguise. Trembling with terror and utterly repulsed, she could not bear even the sight of this personage, and she rushed inside to her private chamber.

Meanwhile, this wicked hermit remained in the sitting room of the family house, conversing with a certain relative of Frances called Paulutio. For he had gained admittance to the house under the pretense of being a venerable person of great holiness and wisdom.

Now, although Frances was safely within the walls of her chamber, she could still mentally see this evil, fake hermit and hear his words. And the counterfeit hermit asked another one of Frances's relatives who was there, a young woman named Vanessa, what was wrong with Frances and where she was. But thankfully, Vanessa suspected that something was amiss and refused to tell him anything. Meanwhile, Frances prayed earnestly, and the demon (disguised as a hermit) suddenly disappeared, harming no one in the household.

Another demonic attack occurred one night while St. Frances, the servant of God, was in her chamber devoutly engaged in her usual sacred exercises. A horrible demon suddenly appeared and seized Frances by her hair, violently raising her from the ground by this means. It dragged her through the air, painfully suspended by her hair, and dangled her over the edge of a balcony that was near her chamber. And then it spoke to her, threatening to drop her to the ground unless she agreed to follow his evil commands. Since the balcony was a high one, such a fall would certainly have caused her to plummet to her death. Frances remained suspended in the precarious and terrifying state for some time, but she placed her faith entirely in the Lord. And after a while, thanks to divine grace working, she found herself suddenly safely positioned again in her chamber, free from all danger.

After this incident, from which she had emerged victorious and unharmed, St. Frances cut short her hair (which, until then, had been exceptionally long and beautiful), as a precaution to avoid any similar assaults in the future.

Another time it happened that Frances, together with her kinswoman, the aforementioned Vanessa, decided to visit the great Basilica of St. John Lateran. Along the way, Frances and Vanessa happened to pass near the Church of St. Peter and St. Marcellinus. As the two women were fatigued by the journey, they sat down upon a stone bench to take some rest.

As they rested, they conversed casually. And as they spoke with each other, the devil, the ancient foe of the human race, approached them! This time he wore the disguise of an elderly man with a very long beard. And he spoke to them thus: "I will ask you just one thing—that you two women should ..." And here, he asked a most disgraceful and indecent thing indeed, which cannot be repeated.

Now, St. Frances had a passionate hatred for all vices and sins, but, above all, she hated depravity of the flesh. Immediately, she recognized the filthy old pervert to be the devil in disguise. And she said to him angrily: "O wicked and contemptible demon! Do you think that I do not recognize you for what you really are? Do you seriously think you can deceive me just by taking on a human form, you miserable wretch?"

At this point, Frances's kinswoman Vanessa was utterly terrified. But the saint said to her: "Do not fear this vile and degenerate creature!" Frances then urged Vanessa to join with her in prayer. Falling to their knees, both of them beseeched the power of the almighty Lord. And, instantly, the demon who had appeared to them vanished into nothingness.

One night, when Blessed Frances was occupied in her customary prayers and vigils in her chamber, a horrible and abominable vision suddenly appeared before her. An evil spirit was there, and it carried with it the body of a dead human being (or perhaps that of another demon, who had disguised itself in the form of a dead human being). This corpse was already decaying and full of worms and emitted a most foul stench. The demon seized Frances and placed her on top of this putrid cadaver, rolling her around violently and forcing her face directly into the foulness of the rotting flesh of the dead body.

Even after the demon had departed, taking with it the decaying corpse, the awful stench remained. The night clothes that Frances wore were pervaded by the smell, which could not be removed, even by hard and repeated washing.

When this incident had occurred, Frances had already been suffering from an infection of the stomach. But afterward, her illness become many times worse. And for a long time, whenever she attempted to eat, the memory of this foul stench of the corpse would come back to her so vividly and overwhelmingly that she was scarcely able to consume anything without nausea and repulsion.

Another circumstance that caused the sensation of this disgusting odor of the decaying cadaver to return to Frances was the presence of any person whose life was infected with the vices of the flesh. The more seriously such a person was inclined toward and enmeshed in these vices, the more strongly did St. Frances experience the foul smell of the corpse in the person's presence.

On another occasion, as St. Frances, the handmaid of God, devoted herself to earnest prayer and sacred meditation at night in her chamber, a certain evil spirit appeared to her. Its face was hideous and filled with hateful rancor. It said to Frances: "Be warned: I shall make your kinswoman Vanessa fall to her death before your eyes!" Having said this, the demon vanished, leaving Frances very anxious about the safety of her beloved relative.

Sometime after this vision had occurred, Frances and Vanessa both planned on attending the liturgy on the anniversary of the dedication of the Basilicas of St. Peter and St. Paul. The two women went forth together at dawn for this purpose. And it happened that, as they descended a certain staircase along the way, Vanessa suddenly fell! She was badly bruised and injured from head to foot. But Frances prayed earnestly to God, and, through the action of divine grace, her kinswoman was healed completely.

Now, the evil spirit who had appeared to Frances had distinctly told her that Vanessa would fall to her death—which, in fact, did not happen at all. And it was clear to Frances, who was able to see angels quite visibly, that a certain angel had intervened while Vanessa was falling to prevent her accident from being fatal.

The devil, the enemy of the human race, very often tormented St. Frances, the servant of God, to the point where she was perplexed at his persistence in evil. On one occasion, she was bold enough to ask the Prince of Darkness a question. "O miserable one, why do you not return to the mercy of God?" she inquired. "Why do you not repent and seek pardon from the good Lord?"

To this, the wicked devil replied: "It is God who should seek pardon from me! For He has done a much greater injury to me that I ever did to Him." To this, St. Frances pointed out to him that it was thanks to his pride that all his woes had befallen him.

But the devil then argued further: "Tell me: Why is it said that the sheep will be placed at the right hand of God and will receive a reward of eternal life, whereas the poor goats will be placed at His left and be sent off to eternal fires? How can this be fair, since neither the sheep nor the goats chose what they are?"

But Frances had a correct and sensible explanation readily at hand. "The goats represent those proud sinners of wicked life, who are rightly punished for their own voluntary actions, just as you are! But the sheep represent those who are humble and obedient to the precepts of God, and do not permit themselves to stray from His divine will." As soon as she had offered this wise reply, the devil was filled with confusion and embarrassment and immediately vanished.

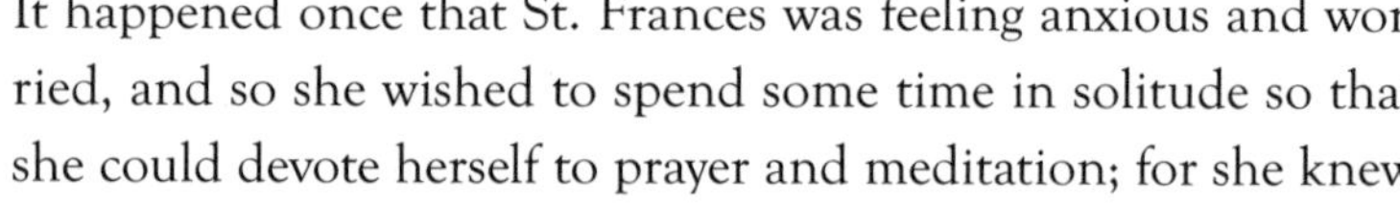

It happened once that St. Frances was feeling anxious and worried, and so she wished to spend some time in solitude so that she could devote herself to prayer and meditation; for she knew that the contemplation of the supreme goodness, perfection, and glory of God was a sure remedy for such feelings. So she went inside her private chamber, carefully closing the door behind her.

But then a demon suddenly appeared to her, this time taking on the disguise of her own trusted spiritual director, Canon Matteotti! He had in his hand a notebook and pen, and he said that he wished Frances to write down the various revelations and visions that she had experienced. Then he said to her: "You should learn to write, Frances, for if you could, you would be able to produce a vast number of magnificent books of all the divine revelations that God has bestowed upon you!"[11]

As this point, however, St. Frances recognized that this was not really her spiritual director at all but the devil concealed beneath a cunning disguise. For she sensed that his request and suggestion were intended to sow within her the seeds of vainglory and the desire for human praise. And so she said to him: "O wretch, you are not really my spiritual director, but a lying and deceptive demon concealed beneath his likeness!"

But the demon persisted in his pretense, saying: "Why do you speak badly to me, Frances, your beloved spiritual father? Remember that I am a minister of God, and with my consecrated hands I hold the Most Holy Sacrament of the Body of Christ. I have come to you so that your wonderful and profound visions may be recorded in writing, so that, after you have passed away, all people shall be able to read about them and will know of your sanctity."

But Frances, who was not to be deceived so easily, then said to him: "You wicked devil, *you* should write down all the wonderful things you saw when you were in the Kingdom of Heaven, before God cast you out and you were damned forever to the fires of Hell!"

As the saint said these words, the devil became furious and could no longer contain himself. Instantly his form changed, and he ceased to bear the likeness of Frances's spiritual father,

[11] At this time, reading and writing were considered and taught as separate skills. Most wealthy and cultured women, such as Frances, were able to read (including in Latin) but were not skilled in writing.

becoming instead a hideous, fire-breathing dragon! This dragon seized Frances and dashed her against the walls for a space of time, before hurling her into the air.

But at last she managed to flee from his jaws, into the upper sunroom of the house. From there, she called out to the dragon: "I do not care about what you have done to me, and if you are capable of inflicting further torments on me, go ahead and do so! For regardless of what you may do to me, I will always despise you and look upon you with contempt."

Upon hearing these words, the dragon seemed to become perplexed and stood still for a while. Then it transformed itself into a human form once more—this time of a man holding a sharp spear in its hand. And he said to the brave saint: "I will kill both you and your son! And so that your pain and suffering will be greater, I will kill your son first while you look on. And only after you have witnessed him die horribly will I kill you!"

But Frances did not lose courage at this threat. She responded to the demon: "You are able to do nothing at all, O wicked creature, except what God permits you to do. So go ahead, and do the worst you can, for I know that God will not allow you to do a deed of such wickedness." At this point, the demon was enraged and projected his spear directly at her. But Frances deftly caught the weapon in her hand. She pulled the head of the spear off, which was about as long as two handspans. Now, this spearhead had been in the form of iron, but as she clasped it firmly in her hand, it become soft and frail, like a scrap of paper!

The combat of Frances with the devil in this case had taken a long time, from about three in the afternoon till sunset. So one of Frances's daughters in the Lord, Rita by name, called out to her to see if anything was wrong. And as soon as she called to her, the demon instantly vanished. Indeed, this was what always happened when anyone called out to Frances while she was being assailed by an evil spirit.

On another occasion, at night, Frances, the handmaid of Christ, was preparing some medicinal items for her husband in her private chamber, for he happened to be seriously ill at that time. And suddenly a wicked demon grabbed her! It carried her off to a veranda of the house under which there was a deep well. And it held her there, suspended in the air, as if it was about to hurl her into the dark depths of the well shaft below. But Frances placed her trust in the Lord completely and cried out fervently: "O my Jesus Christ!" It was indeed her custom to invoke Christ in this manner in times of the greatest peril and anxiety. And, after this prayer, the demon released her so that she was standing safely on the veranda.

Slightly confused at how she had come to be on the veranda at all, Frances then tried to return to her chamber. But she found the door to be firmly locked. She suspected that an evil spirit must be responsible and had perhaps carried her out through the window. Accordingly, she tested the window and found that, while it was closed, it was not latched. So she reentered her chamber through that window.

At this point, she recalled her ailing husband, who was still awaiting her and the medicines he needed. She brought them to him promptly, but he complained about the long delay. Frances was reluctant to reveal to him the strange demonic attack which she had experienced, however, so she simply assured him, with all humility and honesty, that there was no intentional fault or negligence on her part.

One on occasion during the hours of the night, St. Frances was in her chamber engaged in her usual prayers and sacred meditations. Her husband, however, in a sitting room nearby at the time, was earnestly discussing matters of business, such as the management of cattle, buffalo, sheep, and other livestock. Frances could not help overhearing this conversation, for the voice of her husband was loud and strong. Such worldly affairs had always filled the saint with unimaginable tedium, especially when they interrupted her prayer. So she decided to take herself off to the kitchen (which was farther away in the house), so that she could continue her prayers and meditations in quiet.

When she entered the kitchen, it was completely deserted, for no one else was there at that hour. But there was a large quantity of coals that were still burning in the open oven. As Frances knelt to pray, suddenly a demon seized her and held her body aloft over the burning coals!

But the saint once more placed all her trust in the Lord and invoked the most holy name of Jesus lovingly and devoutly. Her prayer was again successful, for she suddenly found herself positioned comfortably in the sunroom of the house, liberated from the burning coals through divine intervention. And she was completely unscathed, although there was a very slight singeing of the tips of her toes.

One night, as St. Frances was in her chamber praying intently, two hideous demons appeared to her. They held in their hands cords or whips fashioned from the sinews of animals, and they beat her viciously with them. As often happened, they then carried her to the veranda of the house and threatened to hurl her from there to the ground below.

But then a third demon appeared, causing the other two to depart immediately. This one was in the form of a giant asp or serpent, and it tried to spit its noxious venom into her face. Indeed, it knew that Frances always had a great abhorrence and fear of snakes of all kinds. But the saint invoked the name of Jesus fearlessly, imploring His divine protection against this terrible foe who attacked her.

At this point, the other two demons who had departed now suddenly reappeared. Thus, Frances was now confronted simultaneously with three malignant enemies, two of whom wished to hurl her to her death, while the third one was trying to spit horrible venom into her face. Aghast and terrified, the saint cried out desperately: "O my Jesus!"

And at once, there was a brilliant flash of radiant light, and the demons all vanished completely. And Frances herself was gently carried in this kindly and glorious light back to the peaceful safety of her own chamber.

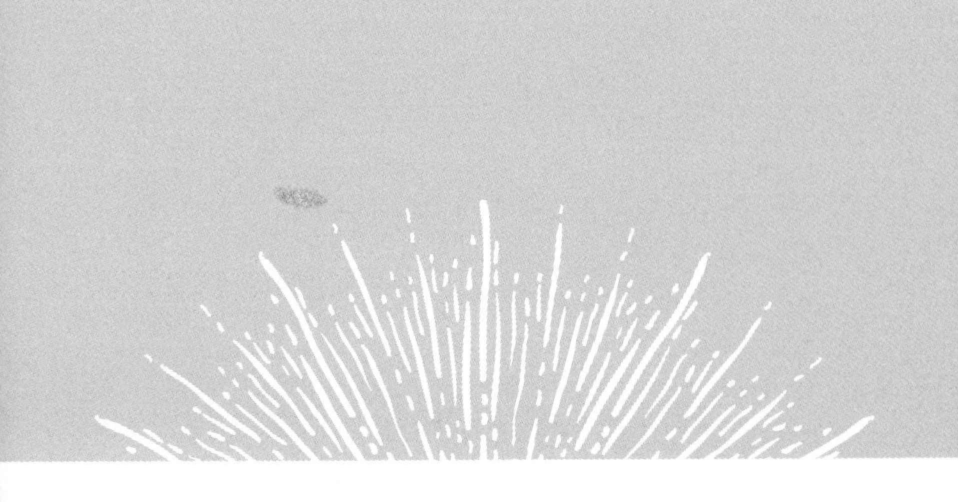

Prayers for after Communion or during Adoration

The Divine Praises

Blessed be God.
Blessed be His Holy Name.
Blessed be Jesus Christ, true God and true Man.
Blessed be the Name of Jesus.
Blessed be His most Sacred Heart.
Blessed be His most Precious Blood.
Blessed be Jesus in the most Holy Sacrament of the Altar.
Blessed be the Holy Spirit, the Paraclete.
Blessed be the great Mother of God, Mary most holy.
Blessed be her holy and Immaculate Conception.
Blessed be her glorious Assumption.
Blessed be the name of Mary, Virgin and Mother.
Blessed be St. Joseph, her most chaste spouse.
Blessed be God in His angels and in His saints.

May the Heart of Jesus in the Most Blessed Sacrament be praised, adored, and loved with grateful affection, at every moment, in all the tabernacles of the world, even till the end of time. Amen.

ANIMA CHRISTI

Soul of Christ, sanctify me;
Body of Christ, save me;
Blood of Christ, inebriate me;
Water from the side of Christ, wash me;
Passion of Christ, strengthen me;
O good Jesus hear me;
Within Your wounds hide me;
separated from You, let me never be.
From the evil one protect me.
At the hour of my death, call me,
And close to You bid me,
That with Your saints,
I may be praising You forever and ever. Amen.

PRAYER AFTER COMMUNION

St. Thomas Aquinas

Sweetest Jesus,
Body and Blood most Holy,
be the delight and pleasure of my soul,
my strength and salvation in all temptations,
my joy and peace in every trial,
my light and guide in every word and deed,
and my final protection in death. Amen.[12]

[12] *The Aquinas Prayer Book: The Prayers and Hymns of St. Thomas*, trans. Robert Anderson and Johann Moser (Manchester, New Hampshire: Sophia Institute Press, 2000).

Litany of the Most Blessed Sacrament

St. Peter Julian Eymard

Lord, have mercy. *Lord, have mercy.*
Christ, have mercy. *Christ, have mercy.*
Lord, have mercy. *Lord, have mercy.*
Christ, hear us. *Christ, graciously hear us.*
God the Father of Heaven, *have mercy on us.*
God the Son, Redeemer of the world, *have mercy on us.*
God the Holy Spirit, *have mercy on us.*
Holy Trinity, one God, *have mercy on us.*
Jesus, Eternal High Priest of the Eucharistic Sacrifice, *have mercy on us.*
Jesus, Divine Victim on the Altar for our salvation, *have mercy on us.*
Jesus, hidden under the appearance of bread, *have mercy on us.*
Jesus, dwelling in the tabernacles of the world, *have mercy on us.*
Jesus, really, truly and substantially present in the Blessed Sacrament, *have mercy on us.*
Jesus, abiding in Your fullness, Body, Blood, Soul, and Divinity, *have mercy on us.*
Jesus, Bread of Life, *have mercy on us.*
Jesus, Bread of Angels, *have mercy on us.*
Jesus, with us always until the end of the world, *have mercy on us.*
Sacred Host, summit and source of all worship and Christian life, *have mercy on us.*
Sacred Host, sign and cause of the unity of the Church, *have mercy on us.*

Sacred Host, adored by countless angels, *have mercy on us.*
Sacred Host, spiritual food, *have mercy on us.*
Sacred Host, Sacrament of love, *have mercy on us.*
Sacred Host, bond of charity, *have mercy on us.*
Sacred Host, greatest aid to holiness, *have mercy on us.*
Sacred Host, gift and glory of the priesthood, *have mercy on us.*
Sacred Host, in which we partake of Christ, *have mercy on us.*
Sacred Host, in which the soul is filled with grace, *have mercy on us.*
Sacred Host, in which we are given a pledge of future glory, *have mercy on us.*
Blessed be Jesus in the Most Holy Sacrament of the Altar, *have mercy on us.*
Blessed be Jesus in the Most Holy Sacrament of the Altar, *have mercy on us.*
Blessed be Jesus in the Most Holy Sacrament of the Altar, *have mercy on us.*
For those who do not believe in Your Eucharistic presence, *have mercy on us.*
For those who are indifferent to the Sacrament of Your love, *have mercy on us.*
For those who have offended You in the Holy Sacrament of the Altar, *have mercy on us.*
That we may show fitting reverence when entering Your holy temple, *we beseech You, hear us.*
That we may make suitable preparation before approaching the Altar, *we beseech You, hear us.*
That we may receive You frequently in Holy Communion with real devotion and true humility, *we beseech You, hear us.*

That we may never neglect to thank You for so wonderful a blessing, *we beseech You, hear us.*
That we may cherish time spent in silent prayer before You, *we beseech You, hear us.*
That we may grow in knowledge of this Sacrament of sacraments, *we beseech You, hear us.*
That all priests may have a profound love of the Holy Eucharist, *we beseech You, hear us.*
That they may celebrate the Holy Sacrifice of the Mass in accordance with its sublime dignity, *we beseech You, hear us.*
That we may be comforted and sanctified with Holy Viaticum at the hour of our death, *we beseech You, hear us.*
That we may see You one day face to face in Heaven, *we beseech You, hear us.*
Lamb of God, You take away the sins of the world, *spare us, O Lord.*
Lamb of God, You take away the sins of the world, *graciously hear us, O Lord.*
Lamb of God, You take away the sins of the world, *have mercy on us, O Lord.*
V. O Sacrament Most Holy, O Sacrament Divine,
R. All praise and all thanksgiving be every moment Thine.

Let us pray: Most merciful Father, You continue to draw us to Yourself through the Eucharistic Mystery. Grant us fervent faith in this Sacrament of love, in which Christ the Lord Himself is contained, offered, and received. We make this prayer through the same Christ Our Lord. R. Amen.

Sophia Institute

Sophia Institute is a nonprofit institution that seeks to nurture the spiritual, moral, and cultural life of souls and to spread the gospel of Christ in conformity with the authentic teachings of the Roman Catholic Church.

Sophia Institute Press fulfills this mission by offering translations, reprints, and new publications that afford readers a rich source of the enduring wisdom of mankind.

Sophia Institute also operates the popular online resource CatholicExchange.com. *Catholic Exchange* provides world news from a Catholic perspective as well as daily devotionals and articles that will help readers to grow in holiness and live a life consistent with the teachings of the Church.

In 2013, Sophia Institute launched Sophia Teachers to renew and rebuild Catholic culture through service to Catholic education. With the goal of nurturing the spiritual, moral, and cultural life of souls, and an abiding respect for the role and work of teachers, we strive to provide materials and programs that are at once enlightening to the mind and ennobling to the heart; faithful and complete, as well as useful and practical.

Sophia Institute gratefully recognizes the Solidarity Association for preserving and encouraging the growth of our apostolate over the course of many years. Without their generous and timely support, this book would not be in your hands.

www.SophiaInstitute.com
www.CatholicExchange.com
www.SophiaTeachers.org

Sophia Institute Press is a registered trademark of Sophia Institute.
Sophia Institute is a tax-exempt institution as defined by the Internal Revenue Code, Section 501(c)(3). Tax ID 22-2548708.